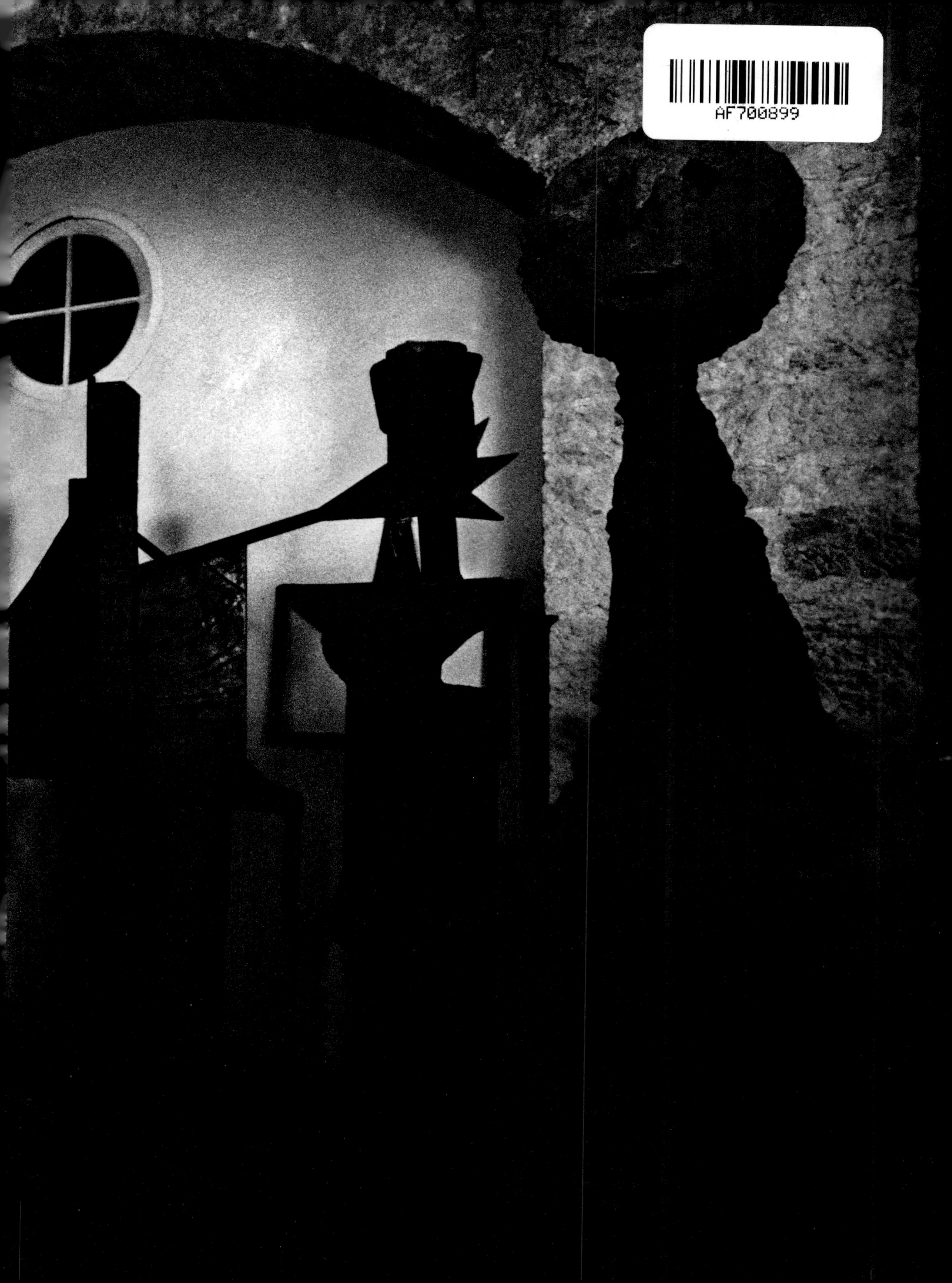

AF700899

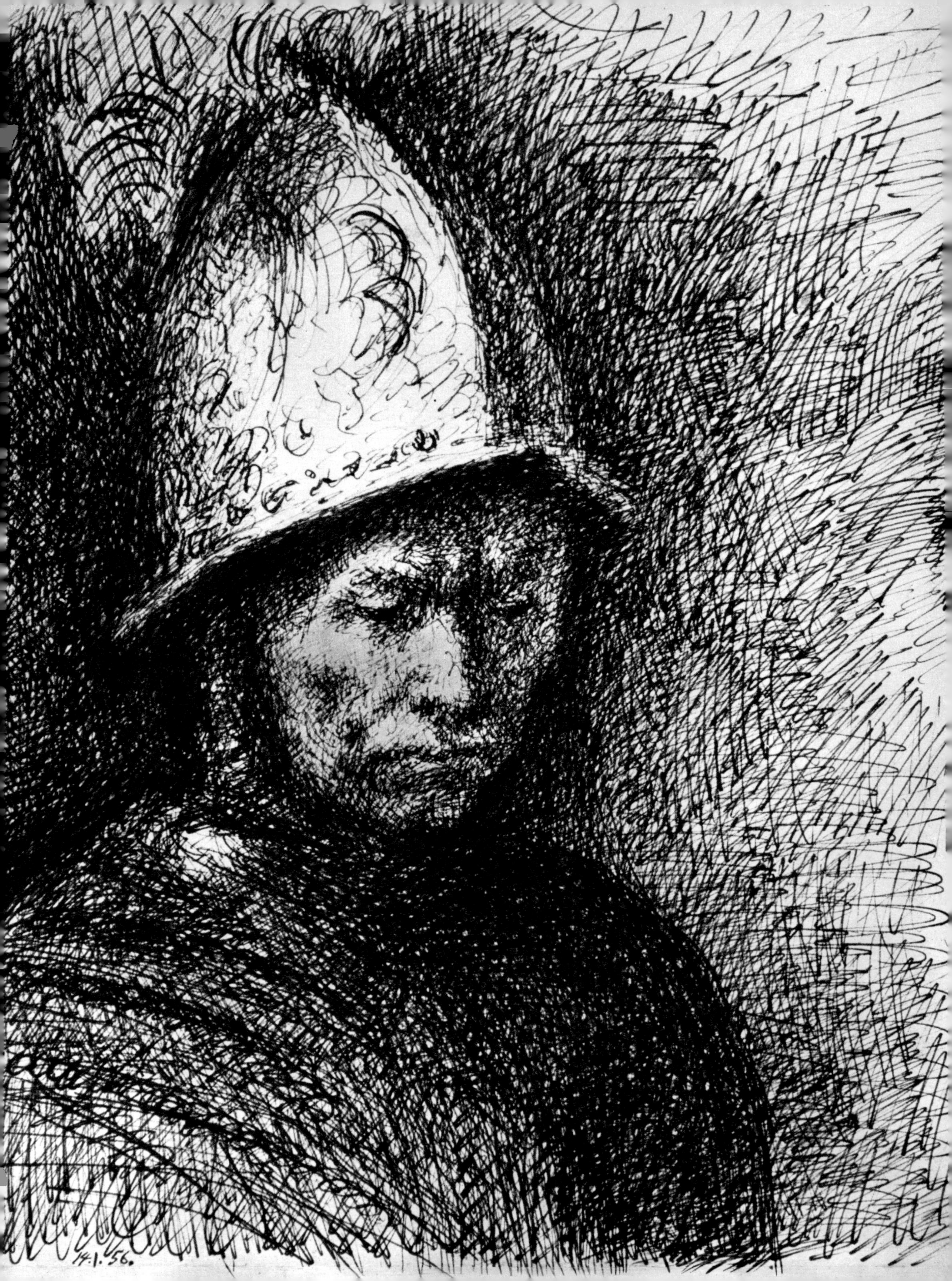
14.1.56.

Pablo
Diego José
Francisco de Paula
Juan Nepomuceno
María de los Remedios
Cipriano de la Santísima Trinidad
Ruiz Picasso

1881 – 1973

self-portrait: 1918

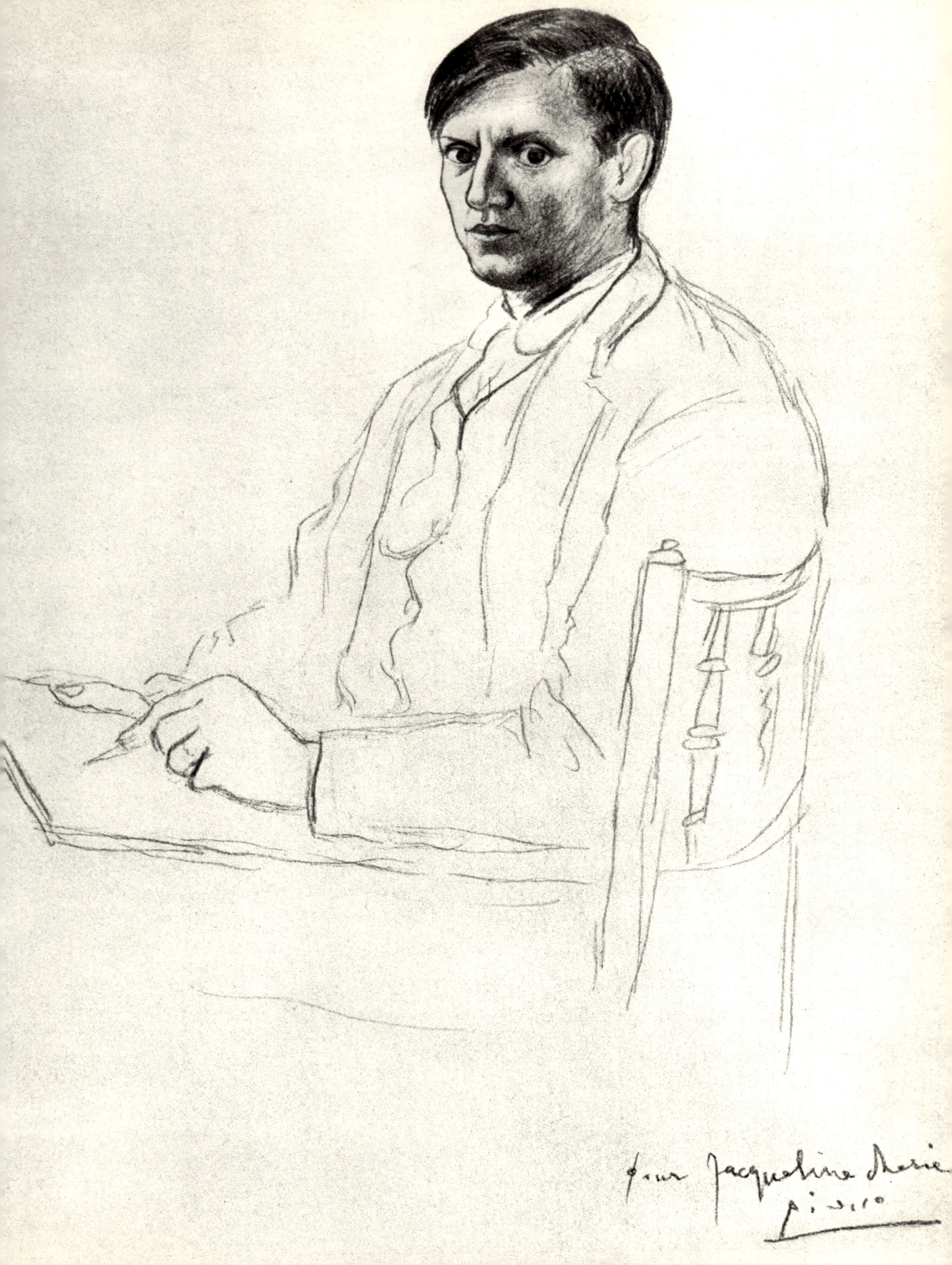

one Sunday morning,
yesterday was forever
in the world
of those who knew him:
the silent studio
was his last self-portrait

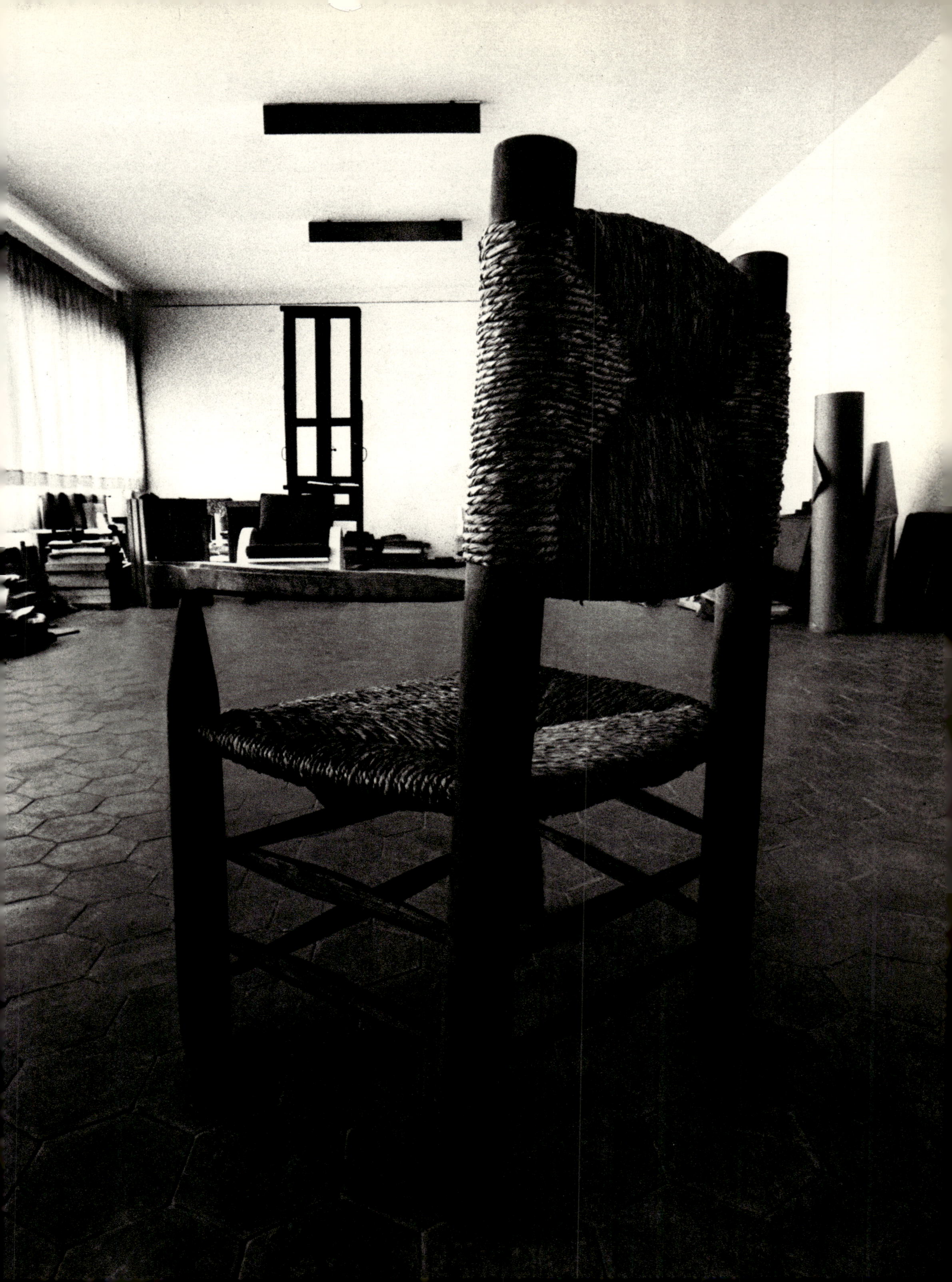

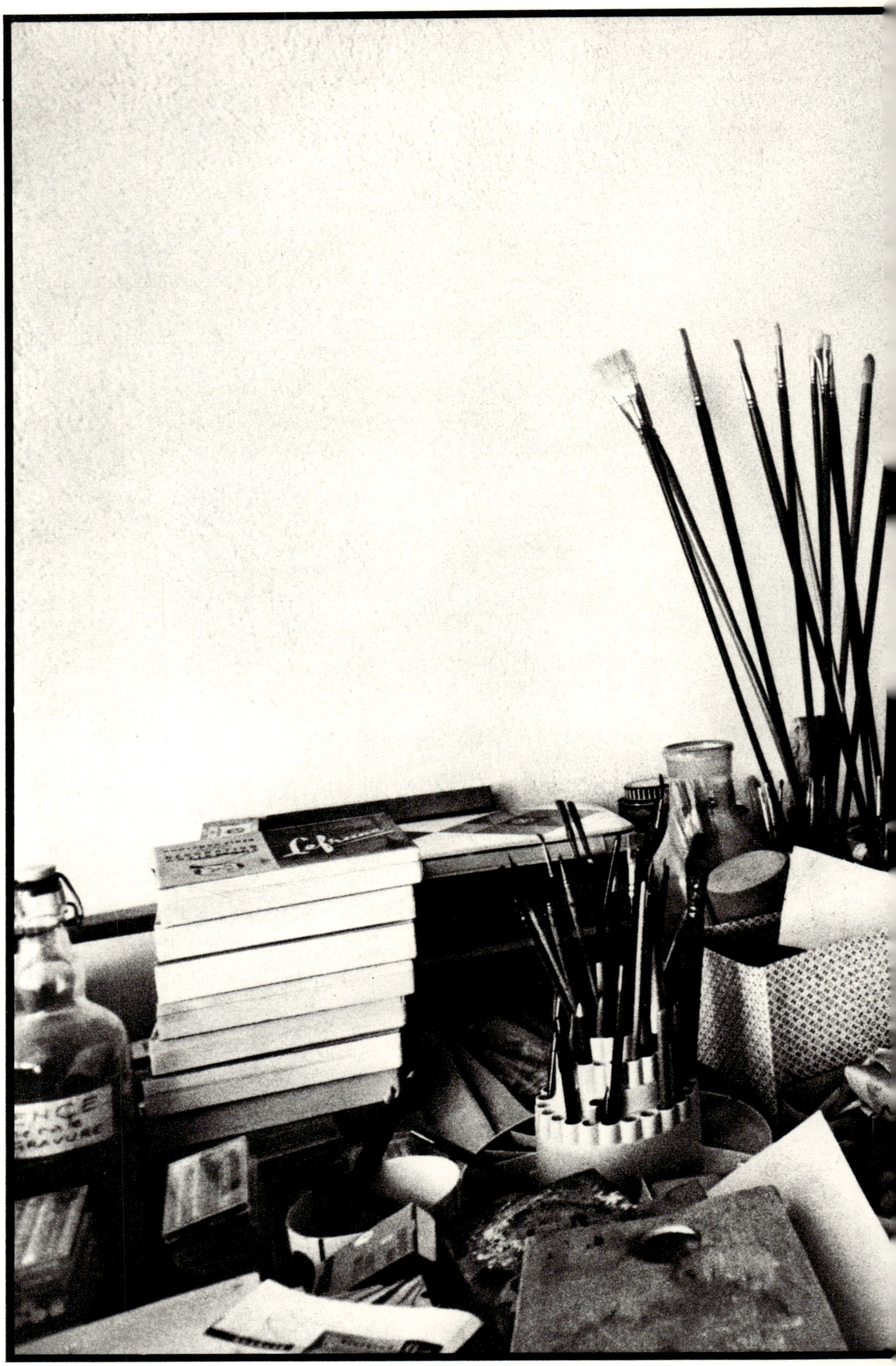

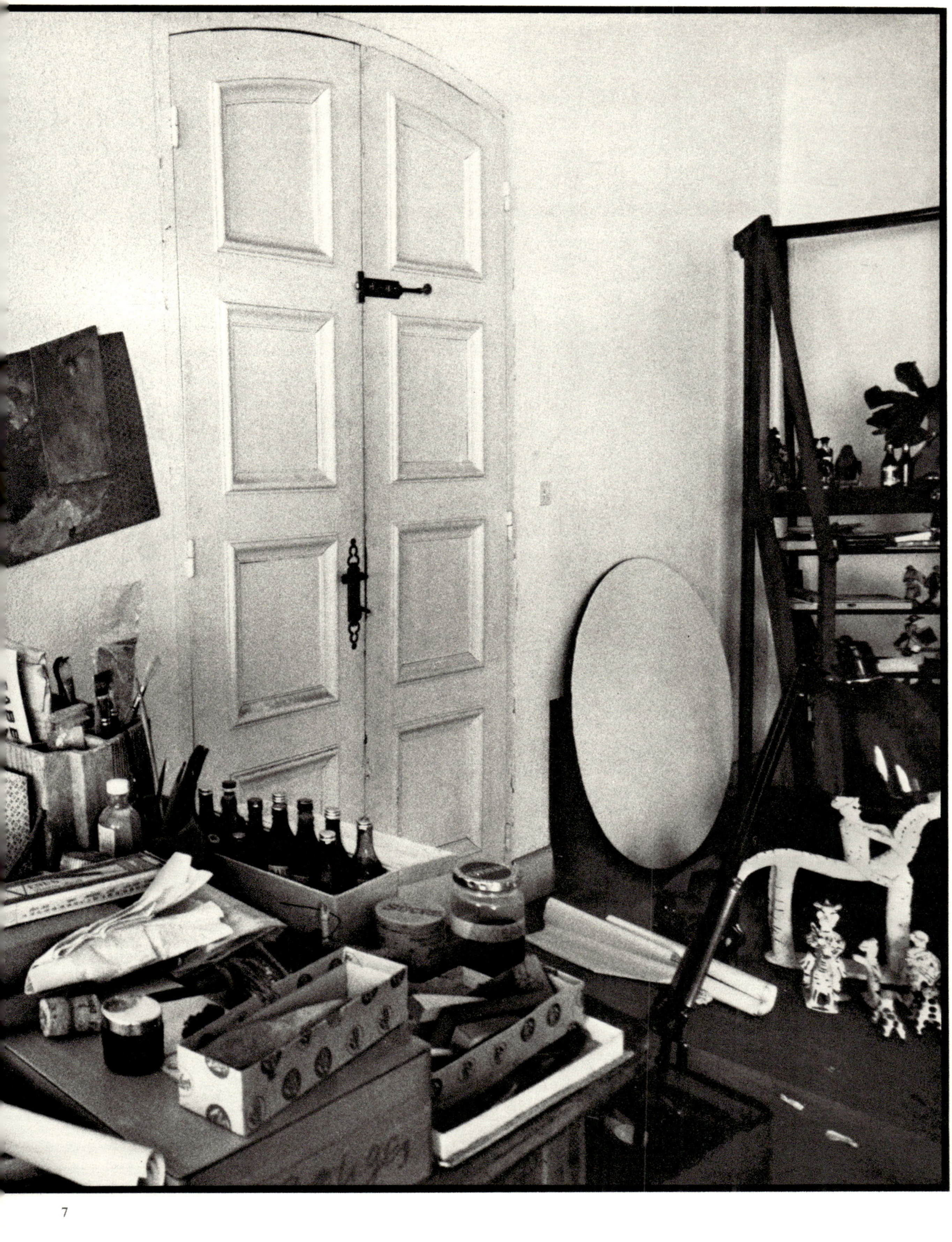

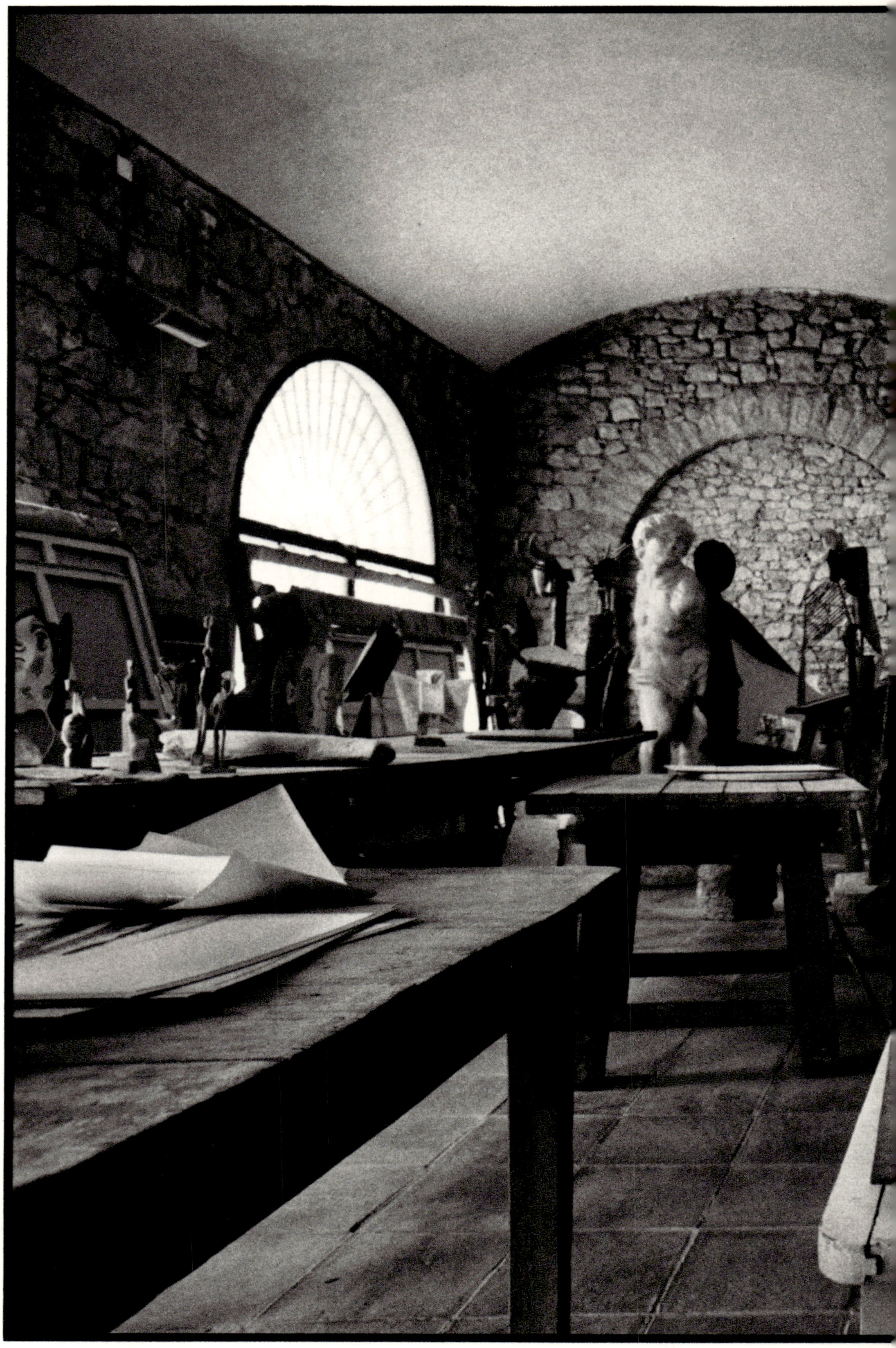

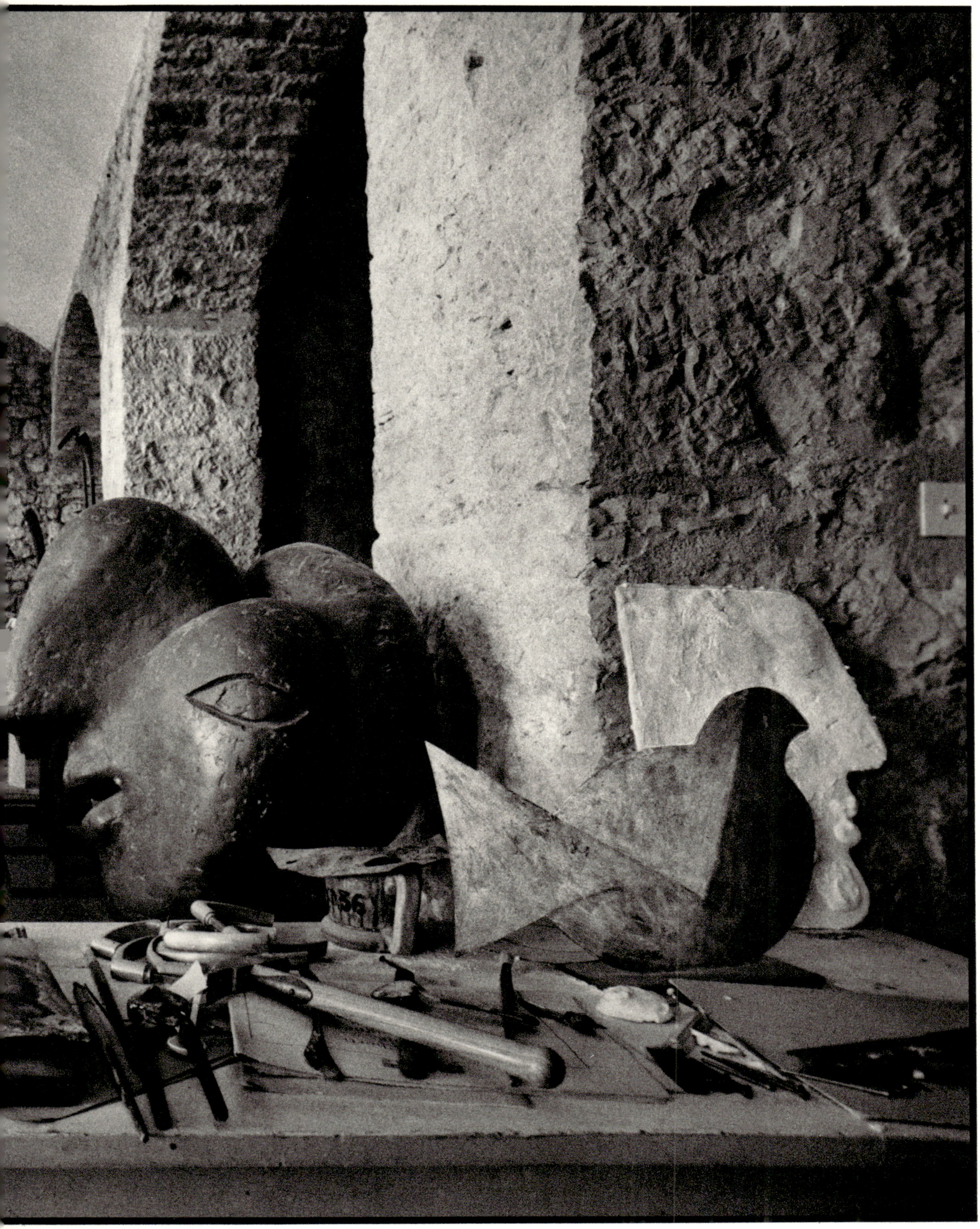

for Jacqueline

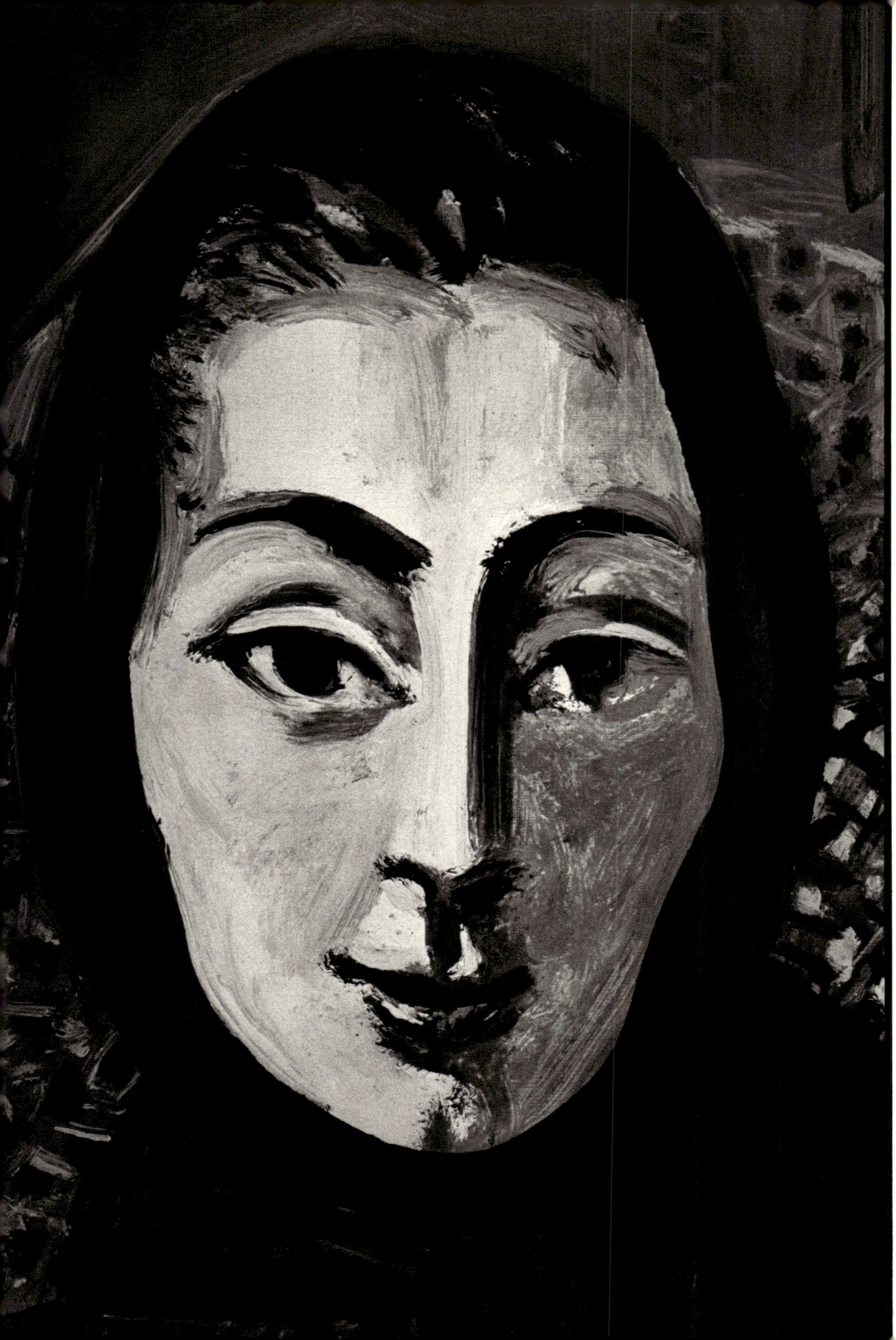

. . . and those
who loved him

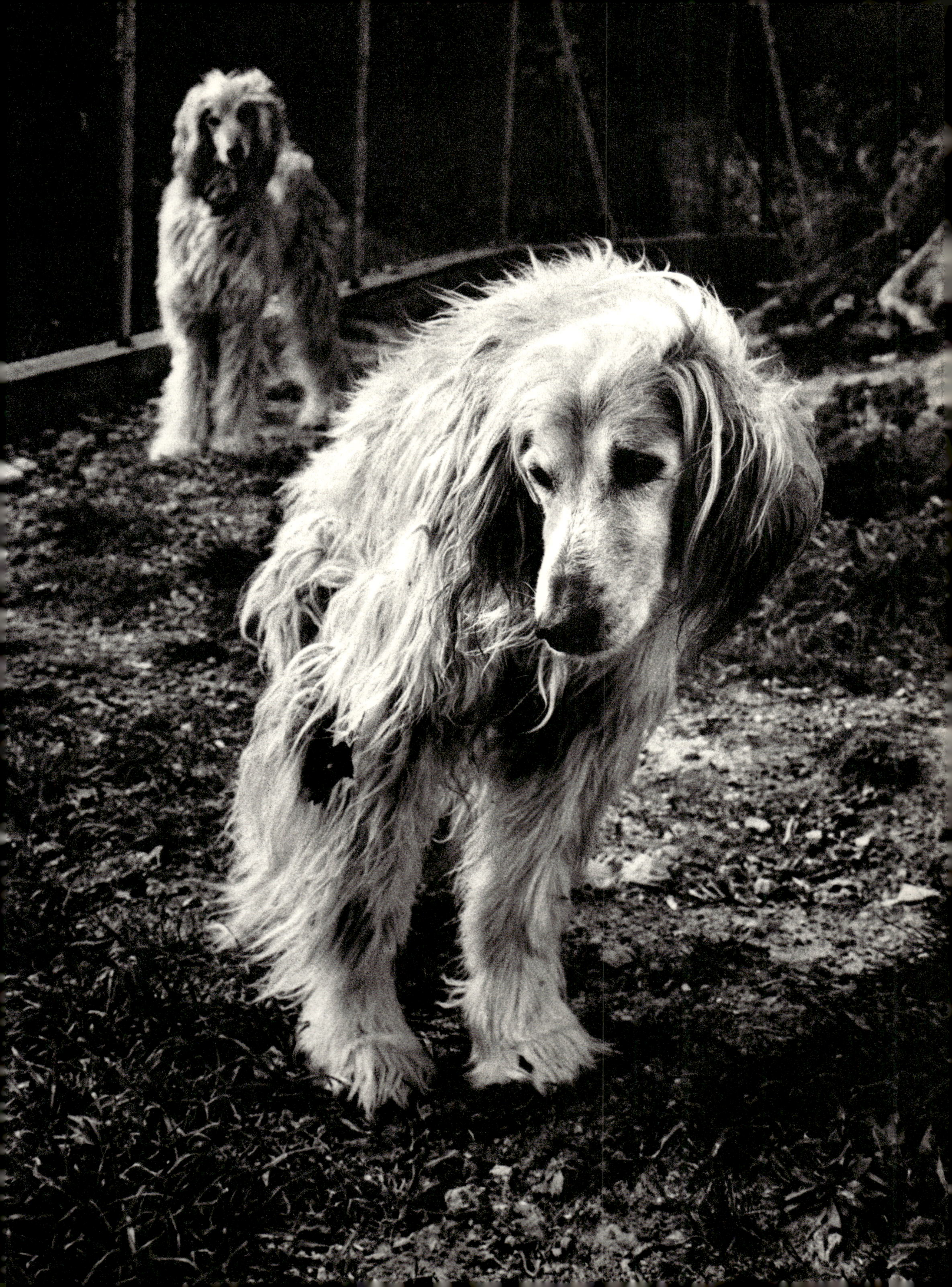

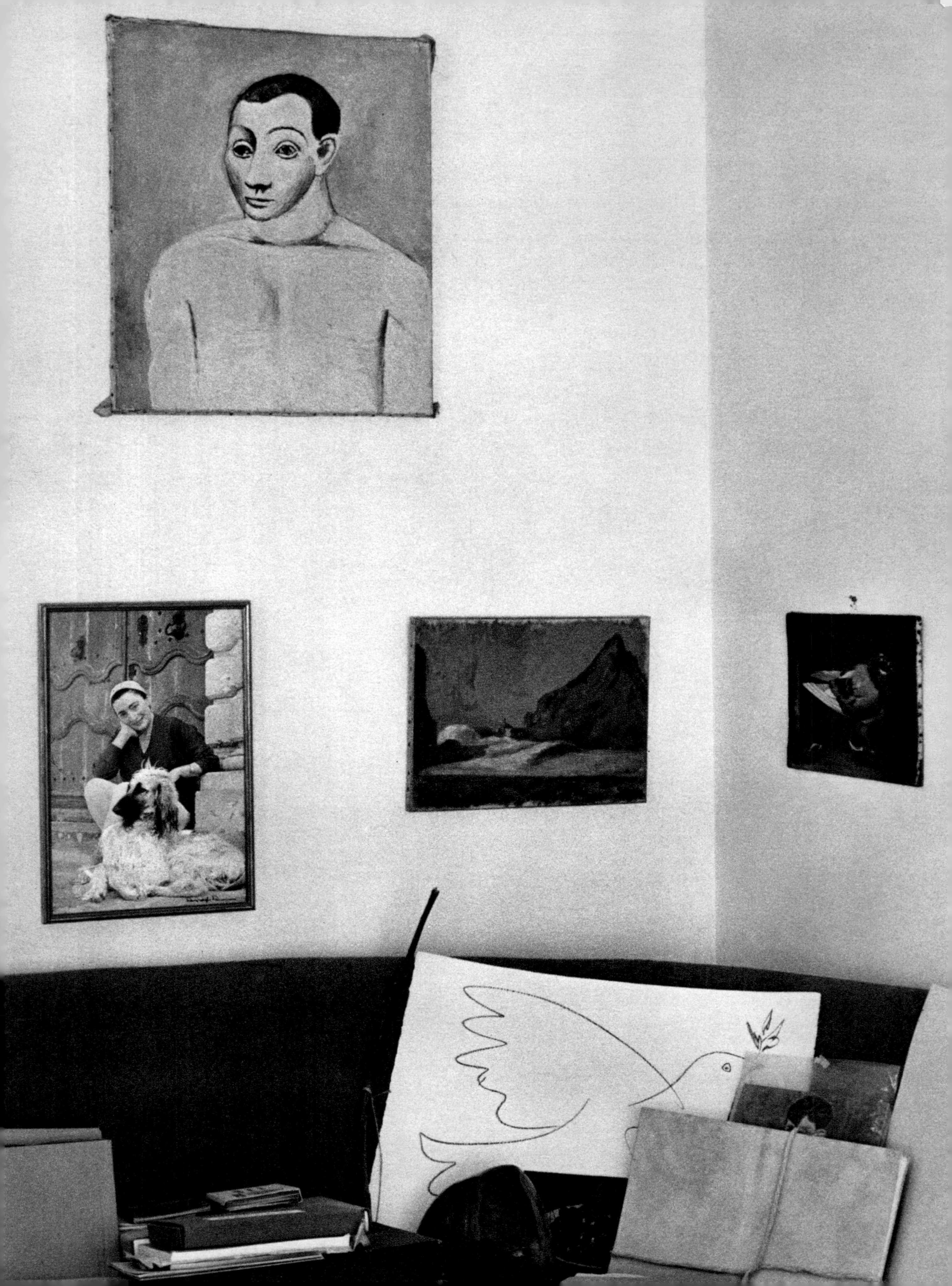

the Silent Studio

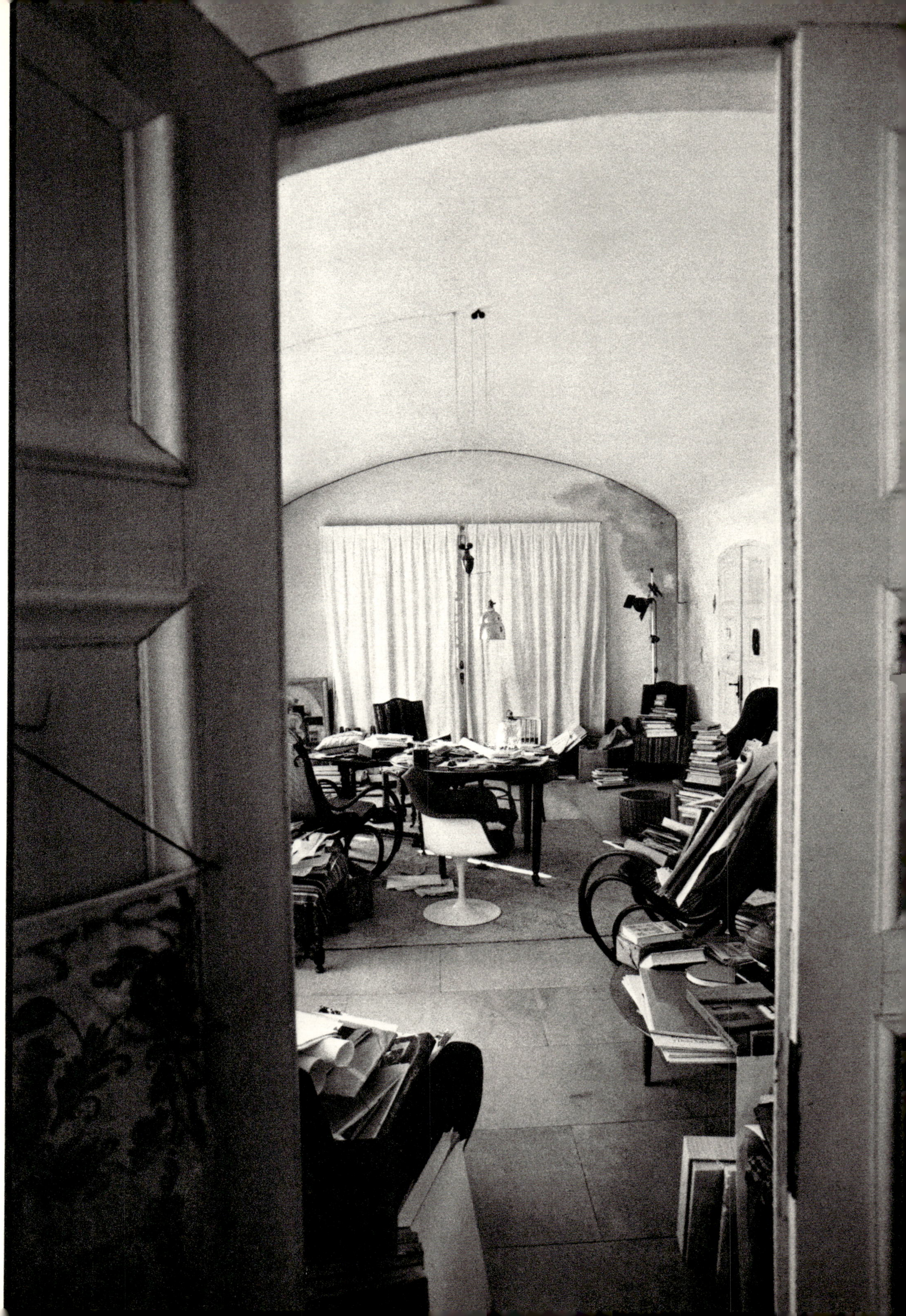

the Silent Studio

David Douglas Duncan

W·W·Norton & Company

photography, text,
design & production
David Douglas Duncan

hand-lettered titles
Gustave Fraass

sheet-fed gravure
Imprimerie Braun SA
Mulhouse-Dornach, France

bindery
Van Rijmenam
The Hague, Holland

published by
W·W·Norton & Company·Inc
500 Fifth Avenue
New York, N.Y. 10036

Copyright 1976
by David Douglas Duncan
All rights reserved

First American edition

Library of Congress
Catalog Number 76-5571
ISBN 0-393-04442-4
Permissions SPADEM

cameras & lenses
Leica M3D
Noctilux 50 mm F/1.2
Leicaflex-SL
Super Angulon 21 mm F/4
Macro-Elmarit 60 mm F/2.8
Angenieux-Zoom 45-90 mm F/2.8
Elmarit 90 mm F/2.8

works by DDD
the Silent Studio
Goodbye Picasso
Prismatics
Portfolio
War Without Heroes
Self-Portrait: USA
I Protest!
Yankee Nomad
Picasso's Picassos
Great Treasures of the Kremlin
The Private World of Pablo Picasso
This Is War!

Contents

The Man in the Golden Helmet, 14-1-56, china ink on paper. 17 x 13 – 43 x 33. From Rembrandt's oil painting (circa 1650) of the same title. *Frontispiece*

Self-portrait, 1918, signed, pencil on paper. 11 1/2 x 9 – 29 x 22.8 (dedicated *"Pour Jacqueline chérie"* and given to her in 1971). Picasso told her he drew this when he learned of the death of his friend, poet Guillaume Apollinaire, at the end of the First World War *(a mirror-reversed image).* *3*

The "viewing" studio, Notre-Dame de Vie. Picasso rarely painted here but spent hours in the old caned chair studying new works stacked along the walls. 201 canvases, painted in a year and a half (1970-72), were trucked from this room to Avignon–his last exhibit–six weeks before he died. *5*

Old and new brushes, boxes of paint, abandoned palettes, etching acids, varnishes and crayons and children's ceramic horsemen–and total silence. A worktable corner of the artist's last studio. *6–7*

North wing of the ground-floor sculpture gallery under Notre-Dame de Vie's main studio. Peasant worktables, tools, sketches, and miscellaneous sheet metal, wood, and bronze sculptures (1931-61) on table at left. (l.r.): Michelangelo's *Rebellious Slave,* 1513-16, plaster copy, against far wall. *Head of a Girl,* 1932, bronze. 50 3/8 x 22 3/4 x 26 – 128 x 58 x 66. *Dove,* 1961, painted sheet metal. 16 x 11 1/2 x 23 3/4 – 40.5 x 29 x 7. *Self-portrait,* 1960, plaster on cardboard. 17 x 11 3/8 x 1/8 – 43 x 31 x 0.5. *8–9*

Jacqueline, 11-10-54, oil on canvas *(detail).* *11*

Kabul, the regal Afghan, spent his last days gazing at the villa as though remembering those early years when he was constantly at the side of Picasso and Jacqueline. He died in the autumn of 1975, shortly after this photograph was taken. Sauterelle, his youthful companion, now shares Notre-Dame de Vie with Igor, the black Afghan from Spain. *13*

A corner of Picasso's last salon. *Self-portrait,* 1906, unsigned, oil on canvas. 25 5/8 x 21 1/4 – 65 x 54. *Snowscape,* 1890s, oil on canvas by Manuel Pallarés, Picasso's oldest friend. *Pigeon,* 1880s, oil on canvas by José Ruiz Blasco, Picasso's painter-professor father. *Peace Dove,* 1951, lithograph. Jacqueline with Kabul at the Château de Vauvenargues, 1962 photograph by DDD. *14*

The artist's salon from the doorway of the painting studio. Beyond the curtained doorway is the viewing studio *(pages 5; 30–31).* *16*

Igor arrived as a puppy after Picasso died, a gift to Jacqueline from her daughter Cathy, who lives in Madrid. He greeted everyone coming to the studio's deceptively modest door; at night he slept outside Jacqueline's bedroom. With patriarchal Kabul gone, he now roams the garden as a lord of the villa, which no one takes seriously–not even Igor. *25*

Olive groves shade Picasso's last studio, which overlooks Mougins on the French Riviera. A nearby pilgrimage chapel, Notre-Dame de Vie, gives the villa its name. Shortly after the artist's death in 1973, Jacqueline found this tiny flock of sheep in her garden–a gift from friends hoping to ease her loneliness. *Man With a Sheep,* one of the artist's most renowned bronzes, appears to guard the little troop being shepherded to its corral. Sculpture gallery is behind the doorways. *28–29*

The flourescent-lit viewing studio was added to the villa soon after Picasso moved to Mougins in 1961. There were 30-odd rooms but he needed more space. Originally this was a flowers-and-fountain patio framing the front door–now eliminated. During the modification period the service entrance served as a front door, and still does. A XIXth-century Baoulé wood sculpture stands beside the arched doorway, behind which was Jacqueline's and Picasso's salon *(next page).* *30–31*

Louis XIIIth banquet chairs, turn-of-the century Austrian rockers, fiberglass Scandinavian bucketseat moderns; museum catalogues, art books, exhibition posters; Blue and Rose Period canvases–and a 1928-29 wire construction dangling from a door lintel–all encircle the table where he welcomed friends with buttered toast and honeyed tea. *32–33*

Jacqueline's garden hat; a sign with which she told Picasso she had "air conditioned" the studio; tiers of books devoted to his work; two Blue Period portraits on the Louis XIIIth sofa–untouched since the day he died. *Mateu de Soto,* 1901-02, unsigned, oil on canvas. 17 3/4 x 14 1/2 – 45 x 37. *Corina Pere Romeu,*

1902, signed, oil on canvas. 23 1/4 x 19 1/4 – 59 x 48.8. Picasso shared his Barcelona studio with de Soto; Corina was the wife of a bistro owner whose *Els Quatre Gats* served Picasso and his painter-poet cronies as a Barcelona command post where they dreamed of conquering the world–Paris. *34–35*

Corina Pere Romeu, 1902, signed, oil on canvas *(detail).* *37*

Picasso's last salon. On the left wall, Blue Period *Roofs of Barcelona,* 1903, unsigned, oil on canvas. 27 3/8 x 43 1/8 – 69.5 x 109.6. Viewing studio is behind camera; painting studio beyond far door. *38–39*

Standing Nude, 1906-07, oil on wooden panel. 26 3/8 x 10 1/2 – 67 x 26.7 (dedicated on verso *"Para Jacqueline el día de su cumpleaños 1970"*. . . "For Jacqueline the day of your birthday 1970"). *40*

His ancient rocker; his "office" of never-answered letters; gifts of the latest crop of art literature; a child's spinner toy, and, protruding from an imperial-size brandy glass, *Figure,* 1907, painted wood. 9 7/8 – 25 (one of Picasso's rarest pre-Cubist sculptures). Photograph of Pablo by Jacqueline. *41*

Self-portrait, 1906, unsigned, oil on canvas *(detail).* *42–43*

Walking Nude, 1906-07, oil on wooden panel. 26 3/8 x 10 – 67 x 25.5 (dedicated on verso *"Para Jacqueline el día de su cumpleaños 1970").* *44*

Wall of salon. *Homage to Picasso on His 90th Birthday,* 1971 watercolor and china ink by Joan Miró (foreground). *La Vanguardia* of Barcelona, which first published the tribute. The artist and Kabul at Vauvenargues, 1962 photo by DDD. Clock-barometer-thermometer gift from admirer *(page 14).* *45*

Peace Dove, 1951, lithograph. Books and unopened parcels overflow the sofa. *46–47*

Window corner of salon. *Parrot and Cage,* 1960, painted ceramic vase made as lamp. Doll, from uranium tycoon–art collector–museum benefactor Joseph Hirshhorn. Gift vases and autumn leaves on radiator. Unshaded light bulb typified Picasso's casual life-style regarding home furnishings. *48–49*

The door between salon and main studio. Picasso's eyeshade for night painting under cinema floodlights, an outdated calendar, books, an embossed Mexican copper plaque, Spanish artist-poet Rafael Alberti's portfolio and a fox hunting horn blend with other special objects to decorate the doorway. *51*

Picasso's salon, door opened to the painting studio, as when he worked in the afternoon. *52–53*

The great painting studio of Notre-Dame de Vie – without Picasso. *54–55*

Picasso's studio table: unshaded light bulb, wax-apple candle, new brushes and tubes of paint; crayons, pencils, varnishes–and a hand-written note on a stack of faded paint boxes "Bought in 1905 with money paid by Gertrude Stein for the first picture she got from me." *56–57*

Just shadows on a wall, an abandoned easel, the never-used fireplace, two Spanish-gourd maracas above a Gothic chest and a child's ornate make-believe cabinet . . . all framed in silence. *58–59*

South wing of ground-floor sculpture gallery. (l-r): *Girl Skipping Rope,* 1950, made of wicker vineyard baskets, a cookie mold, old shoes, metal beams, plaster and ceramic fragments–later cast in bronze. 60 1/4 x 24 7/16 x 25 5/8 - 153 x 62 x 65. Medieval door in background brought to villa by Picasso. *Woman With Vase,* 1933, bronze. 87 1/4 - 222 (undated memo on neck is signed by P. Ruiz Picasso, Jacqueline and two witnesses: "This sculpture belongs to the Spanish Republic." An identical casting stands today atop the artist's grave at his Château de Vauvenargues). Michelangelo's *Dying Slave,* 1513-16, plaster. *60–61*

The entire wing of the sculpture gallery. Plaster copy of Michelangelo's *Dying Slave* towers over plaster cast of *Bust of a Woman,* 1932, the top part of *The Man With a Sheep,* 1944, and miscellaneous other plaster casts. Blank canvases lean against doorways opening on villa's garden. Michelangelo's *Rebellious Slave* (far wall) spotlighted by late afternoon sunlight. Both of the *Slaves* in Picasso's Mougins studio were gifts from the Antibes Grimaldi Palace Museum. *62–63*

Bird, 1961, painted sheet steel. *Self-portrait,* 1960, plaster on cardboard *(pages 8–9).* *65*

Head of a Girl, Bird, and *Self-portrait (pages 8–9).* *66–67*

Notre-Dame de Vie's sculpture gallery grotto with Louis XIIIth table and chairs, and filled with Picasso's work. (l-r): *Girl Skipping Rope,* 1950, bronze *(pages 60–61). Woman with Baby Carriage,* 1950, bronze. Made of a palm frond, kitchen stove burner grids, biscuit cutters, tile pipe, plaster and baby carriage–then cast in bronze. 80 x 75 1/8 x 23 5/8 - 203 x 145 x 60. Pablo and Jacqueline received special dinner guests here, followed by coffee in the first-floor viewing studio, or the salon. *68–69*

South end sculpture gallery grotto with Michelangelo's *Dying Slave* in background. *Mother Baboon and Baby,* 1952, bronze. Originally made of two toy autos (head), coffee cup handles (ears), ceramic bowls (body), a broken car spring (tail) and plaster. 21 5/8 x 13 3/8 x 24 3/4 – 55 x 34 x 63. *Sylvette,* 1954, painted sheet steel. 27 1/8 x 17 1/4 – 69 x 44 *(lower left). Head of Goat,* 1950, plaster *(in bronze vase). Girl Skipping Rope (pages 68–69). Woman with Apple,* 1943, bronze. Original work made of cookie cutter, corrugated paper, tree branch and cake pan–then cast in bronze. 70 7/8 x 30 3/4 x 28 – 180 x 78 x 71 *(right).* *70–71*

Inner corner of sculpture gallery. (l-r): *Standing Girl,* 1953, painted wood. 35 1/2 x 7 1/4 x 2 3/4 – 90 x 18.5 x 6.5. *Standing Girl,* 1953, painted wood. 54 x 17 3/4 x 6 7/8 – 137 x 45 x 17.5. *Mother Baboon and Baby (pages 70–71).* XVIIIth-century Provençal cupboard in background. *72–73*

North end of sculpture gallery wing. (l-r): *Pierrot,* 1961, painted and welded sheet steel. 53 1/4 x 20 1/2 x 18 7/8 – 135 x 52 x 48. Michelangelo's *Rebellious Slave,* 1513–16, plaster copy. Maquette for Chicago's Civic Center *Figure,* 1964, welded steel, painted face. 41 3/8 x 27 1/2 x 18 7/8 – 105 x 70 x 48 (Chicago's *Figure* stands over 60 feet high). Picasso made a gift of his work to the city. *74–75*

Painted sheet-steel figures in sculpture gallery *(page 69). Mother and Child,* 1961, 17 1/4 x 6 7/8 – 44 x 17.5 (average height of group). Scale can be judged by cigarette can on crate. XIXth-century African mask. With imagination this assemblage resembles *Adoration of the Magi.* *76–77*

Central grotto sculpture gallery, next to dinner table *(page 71). Bearded Man,* 1961, painted and welded sheet steel. 16 1/8 x 11 7/8 – 41 x 30. *Woman* (Jacqueline without question), 1961, painted and welded sheet steel. 19 3/4 x 15 3/4 – 50 x 40 (average height of all sheet-steel portraits in this group). Cartoons of these works were cut first from cardboard, then sheet steel. *78–79*

Jacqueline, 2-6-54, oil on canvas. 39 3/8 x 31 7/8 – 100 x 81. Picasso's first work of her. Titled *Portrait of Lady "Z"* years ago by someone who prophesied correctly that she would be his last love. (Dedicated on verso *"pour Jacqueline 25-4-67").* Her impact was immediate and profound. *80*

Jacqueline, 3-6-54, oil on canvas. 45 5/8 x 35 – 116 x 89. *81*

Jacqueline in Rocking Chair, 5-10-54, charcoal and gouache on canvas. 36 1/4 x 28 3/4 – 92 x 73. *82*

Jacqueline in Rocking Chair, 9-10-54, oil on canvas. 57 1/8 x 45 1/4 – 145 x 115 (dedicated verso *"Este cuadro es para Jacqueline con muchos besos mas"*. . . "This picture is for Jacqueline with many kisses more"). *83*

Jacqueline in Black Scarf, 11-10-54, oil on canvas. 36 1/4 x 28 3/4 – 92 x 73 (dedicated recto to Jacqueline at upper left). Closeups of this canvas are on the book jacket and dedication page. *84*

Jacqueline as Turkish Bride, 20-11-55, oil on canvas. 39 3/8 x 31 7/8 – 100 x 81. Hungarian cap, English hair scarf, Turkish jacket: this was the only time Jacqueline posed for a Picasso portrait. *85*

Jacqueline in Candy-wrapper Dress, 13-2-57, charcoal on canvas, and collage of ribbon and paper from box of chocolates, a gift of Swiss art dealers and old friends, Siegfried and Angela Rosengart *(detail).* *86*

Jacqueline as Arlesienne Bride, 8-7 – 15-8-58, oil on canvas. Painted with a dove feather *(detail).* *87*

Jacqueline as Sphinx, 3-4-60, oil on canvas. 36 1/4 x 28 3/4 – 92 x 73. *88*

Jacqueline, 13-12-62, oil on canvas. 39 3/8 x 31 7/8 – 100 x 81. *89*

Jacqueline with Kitten, 24-2-64, oil on canvas. 51 1/4 x 38 1/4 – 130 x 97 (dedicated recto at upper left *"A Jacqueline pour sa fête"*. . . "To Jacqueline for her birthday"). *90*

Jacqueline with Kitten, 26-2-64, oil on canvas. 76 3/8 x 50 3/8 – 194 x 128 (dedicated recto). *91*

Jacqueline, 4-4-64, oil on canvas. 39 3/8 x 31 7/8 – 100 x 81. *92*

The Cavalier Artist, 1967, oil on canvas. 32 1/8 x 25 5/8 – 81.5 x 65. *93*

Pegasus, Nude Girl and Laurel-wreathed Child, 26-28-29-7-72, gouache, china ink and watercolor (dedicated on verso *"Para Jacqueline 15-9-72").* It seems fitting that one of Pablo's last gifts to her should be Pegasus, mythological messenger of poetic inspiration. By comparing the china-ink black of *"28-29"* in the date, one sees where Picasso continued work begun on the 26th, when he used transparent colors for the nude, and slate gray and luna-moth green for the wings of Pegasus. 12 1/2 x 17 3/8 – 31.5 x 44. *94–95*

Cloaked Cavalier, 20-9-72, china ink on paper, a half-page torn from Picasso's sketchbook. 12 1/8 x 8 1/4 – 30.8 x 21 (dedicated verso *"Pour Jacqueline").* With elbow raised and hand on a sword barely concealed by his flowing cape, the *Cavalier* momentarily looks back but keeps striding toward unknown adventures ahead. Anyway, that's how I see it. His last present to Jacqueline was a sheet of paper on which he had painted one word, *"Regalo"*... "Gift." It was her birthday. He died six weeks later. *97*

The silent and empty studio of Notre-Dame de Vie. *98*

Jacqueline nearly perished after Picasso died Sunday noon, April 8th, 1973. For two years she languished in total seclusion, though forced to alternate between Notre-Dame de Vie (where her presence was required as principal heir of the artist's excruciatingly complex estate) and the Château de Vauvenargues (where Pablo is buried and where she dreams of spending the remainder of her life). Many friends tried to help. Few ever saw her. One couple succeeded where all others failed: Jean Chevrier and his wife, Marie Bell, both renowned in the French theater. With their unfailing concern and humor and love, Jacqueline began to improve. Marie Bell thrust Julio, a four-month old, moist-bellied, finger-gnawing dachshund puppy into Jacqueline's arms and this simple contact breached the fortress of her misery. Sitting barefoot in the windowless center of the villa, Jacqueline clutched Julio to her heart and stared into the past–but began to accept the future. Jean and Marie Bell were constant house guests through the spring, summer and into the winter of last year, 1975 . . . when Jean died just before Christmas. Marie Bell now spends many days at Notre-Dame de Vie–where Jacqueline Picasso is striving to find answers for tomorrow, for them both. My photographs were taken that Easter when Jean, Marie Bell and Julio rescued Jacqueline. *100–105*

Self-Portrait, 3-4-64, oil on canvas. 39 3/8 x 31 7/8 – 100 x 81. Painted nine years before his death, the picture raises memories of his 1906 Gertrude Stein portrait which disturbed her as not looking like her. He is said to have replied, "You will." Perhaps he would look like this–reflecting Jacqueline's eyes–today. *106*

Christ, 29-7-71, oil on canvas. 36 1/8 x 28 5/8 – 91.8 x 72.8 (dedicated on verso *"Pour Jacqueline Picasso").* This, for me, was the centerpiece of Pablo's exhibit which opened at Avignon six weeks after he died. It was returned to Jacqueline before thieves looted the Palais des Papes of over one hundred canvases. *107*

Picasso at the door of his Château de Vauvenargues, 1962 photograph by DDD. A print was loaned to the 1964 Japanese Picasso retrospective where it was enlarged and used as an exhibit poster. This poster has been in Notre-Dame de Vie from that time. Since Pablo's death, Jacqueline has kept flowers at its side. Striking similarities are seen when comparing it to *Self-portrait (page 3).* *108–109*

Man With a Sheep, 1944, bronze. 86 1/2 x 30 3/4 x 28 3/8 – 220 x 78 x 72. The doorway to the sculpture gallery, closed and locked. Notre-Dame de Vie has ceased to exist as a studio. *110*

Igor, bored and alone, plays with a black ant patrolling the empty driveway. *Back endpaper*

Note:

The studio of Notre-Dame de Vie

The basic unwritten code governing all photography in the studio-homes of Pablo Picasso was clear and simple; inflexible: Do Not Move *Anything!* Naturally, it was honored when making these photographs in Notre-Dame de Vie. All negatives are full-frame except where the book required full-bleed vertical pages. European (Picasso) method used for all data: vertical–horizontal; inches–centimeters; day–month–year.

Preface

Twenty years ago, venturing into the realm of Pablo Picasso with my camera, I was shown a dusty portfolio of his earliest unknown works. There were pencil sketches of doves and bullfighters and rogues, and Christ giving absolution to the Devil. Nearby, I also saw a newly created pen-and-ink masterpiece inspired by a simple postcard: Rembrandt's brooding portrait of *The Man in The Golden Helmet,* painted around 1650. Picasso had drawn his private version of it in January, 1956, three weeks before our first meeting at La Californie, his home above Cannes on the French Riviera. At that time, Picasso's Rembrandt was wedged into a cluttered chair next to the dinner table which served as a convenient horizontal easel during many of those happy years in the villa. Now, two decades later, I have gone exploring once more at the end of the rainbow in my friend's world–today at Notre-Dame de Vie, his final studio-home above Mougins, the hill town between Cannes and Grasse. And it held many joyous memories, as had La Californie–and also his Château de Vauvenargues near Aix-en-Provence–of children, pets, famed guests and work, work, work when Pablo and Jacqueline and I were alone.

For ten days I found myself again surrounded by the myriad treasures of Notre-Dame de Vie. I was there, this time, as the official documentary photographer for the artist's heirs (Jacqueline, his children Maia, Claude, Paloma and two grandchildren); the court art expert appraising the value of every object in that vast estate, and for the federal tribunal's administrator–the French government itself. Jacqueline was upstairs the entire time. She appeared when her health permitted or when she was needed urgently by the experts, who were assisted by four art historians well into their second year of discovery among the galaxies of Picassos encircling us all. Everyone tried to shield Jacqueline from the obvious agony of having professionals, court-ordered, inside her home cataloguing *everything,* even the contents of Pablo's and her clothes closets. Only rarely was a voice heard in that enormous house, then it was muted. The experts have now returned to Paris. Now it's over. She seems so relieved and exhausted. Everyone who was there shares her feelings–but with an added sense of exhilaration at having seen so much, and, for just a moment at least, being near the heart of a unique man. This accounted for some of the silence. We all cared.

Another voice echoed in my memory: I was roaming again in those vaulted rooms where Picasso's presence seemed constantly to be at my shoulder while he worked too, the way it had been from the beginning. Of all the gifts showered upon me during those years, his friendship and trust were of course the greatest. Nothing changed even after I feather-dusted, before photographing, the secret hoard of "Picasso's Picassos" in the attic of La Californie–and ruined his monumental but unfixed charcoal self-portrait of 1938 by smearing his features clear across the canvas. Since there apparently is no photographic coverage in depth on the studios of any of the other "greats" of our art era following their deaths–Van Gogh, Cézanne, Klee, Matisse, Giacometti, Braque–I want to offer others who care a leisurely visit without words to the studio of a man who enriched my life. Picasso would have shrugged, *"Es su casa"* . . . "It's your home."

One morning in Notre-Dame de Vie I rediscovered the original Picasso-Rembrandt of *The Man in The Golden Helmet,* seen at Villa La Californie that first morning of my friendship with Pablo and Jacqueline. This time I committed the forbidden. I caressed the surface of the work trying to understand the secret of its velvet warmth. I learned nothing. The paper felt... luminous! It is included here. The studio itself will soon be only a memory of what it was one April morning, when Pablo died. Today the inventory is complete. The rooms where he reigned have been invaded. All is orderly desolation. No freshly splattered paint flowers the unwaxed floors. Ever fewer of his sculptures loom in the ground-floor stone-arched gallery shadows awaiting their turn in the transporter's truck. His still-untouched salon has been permitted to survive as a locked semi-shrine–even for the government's meticulous task force. They are reluctant to tag any object in that last room. But its time of grace is shortening. It could be a matter of weeks. Or just days. Jacqueline still lives at Notre-Dame de Vie. Her days in that quiet place are numbered too.

Jacqueline's world fragmented when Pablo died. For the first two years it seemed that she would never survive her heartbreak. My photographs of her, taken when she was near the end of her physical resources, tell something of her loss. She has permitted their publication as *"la verdad"*–the truth–which takes another kind of courage, for they do not flatter a face that inspired Picasso to paint what one day may be viewed as the most haunting portrait of our century. I have chosen it for the jacket and dedication page of this book, which also includes the full series of portraits that he gave to her. In black-and-white, the design of each painting becomes visible–color often camouflages structure. These canvases have never been seen together outside the studio. They span Pablo's and Jacqueline's years together and reveal that his was a love story in paint.

To the last day of his life.

Easter morning
18 April, 1976
Castellaras, France

today, at Notre-Dame de Vie,
Jacqueline's flock of sheep
grazes beneath olive trees
of a studio now locked,
while Igor appears to watch
for someone he never knew

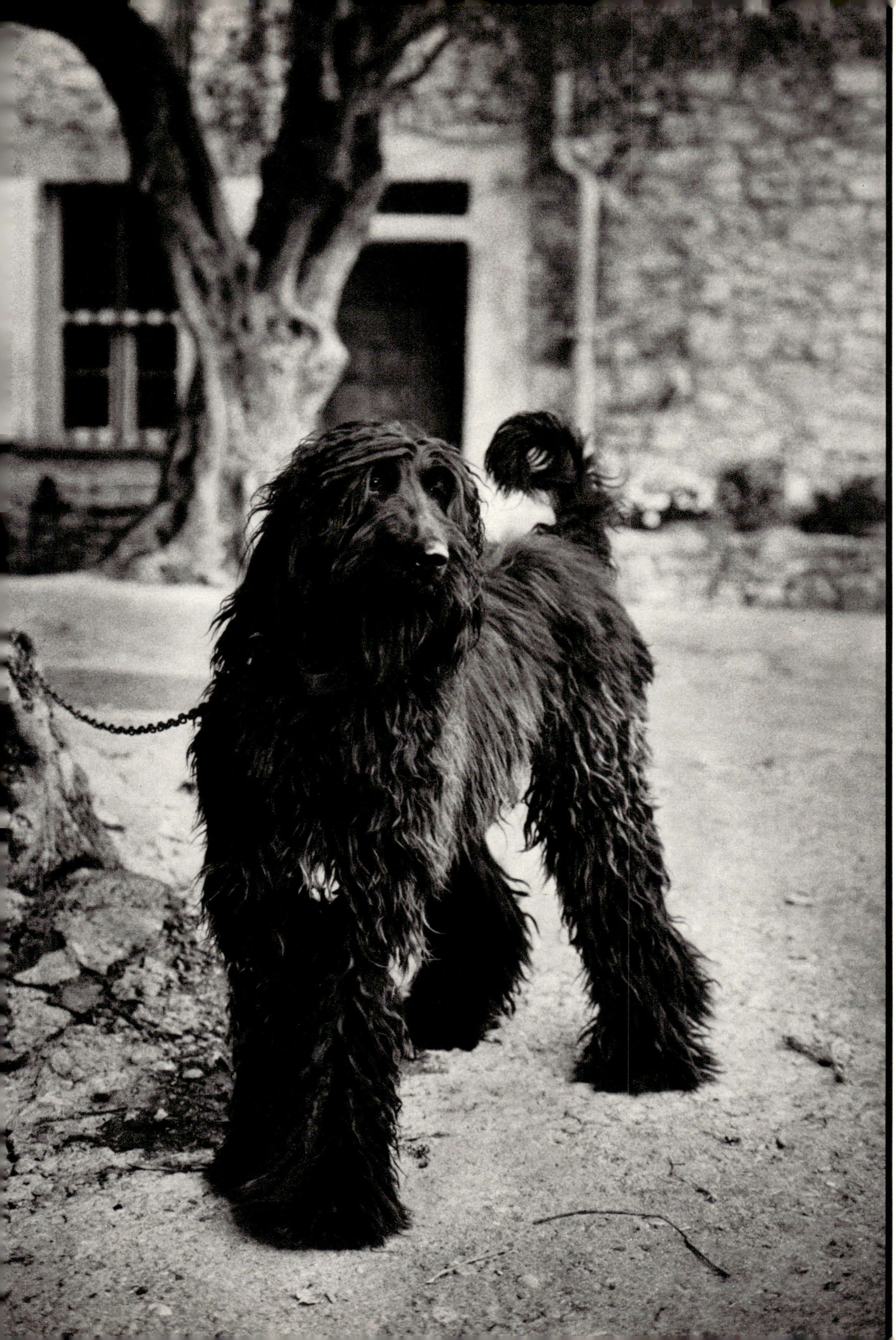

Notre-Dame de Vie

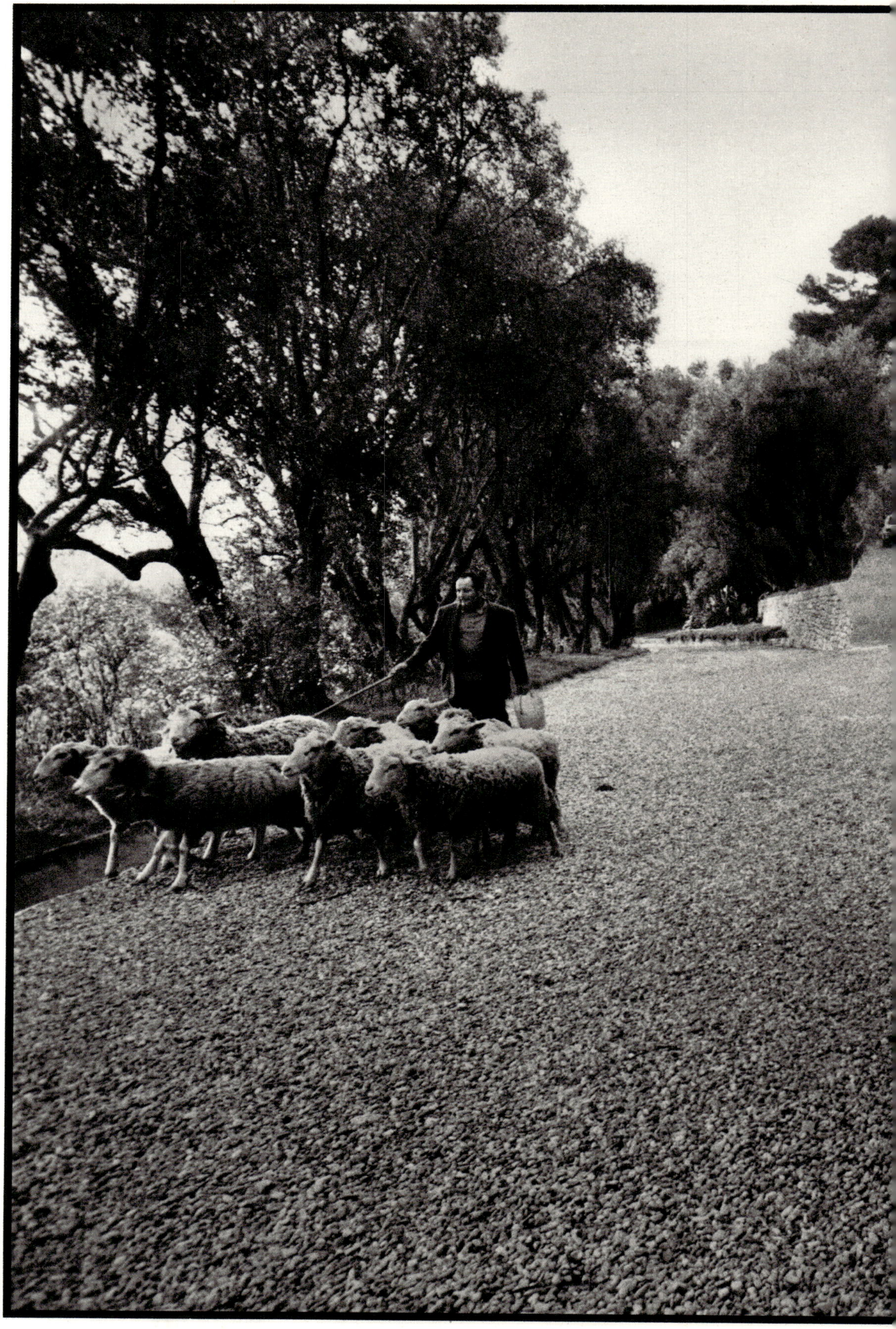

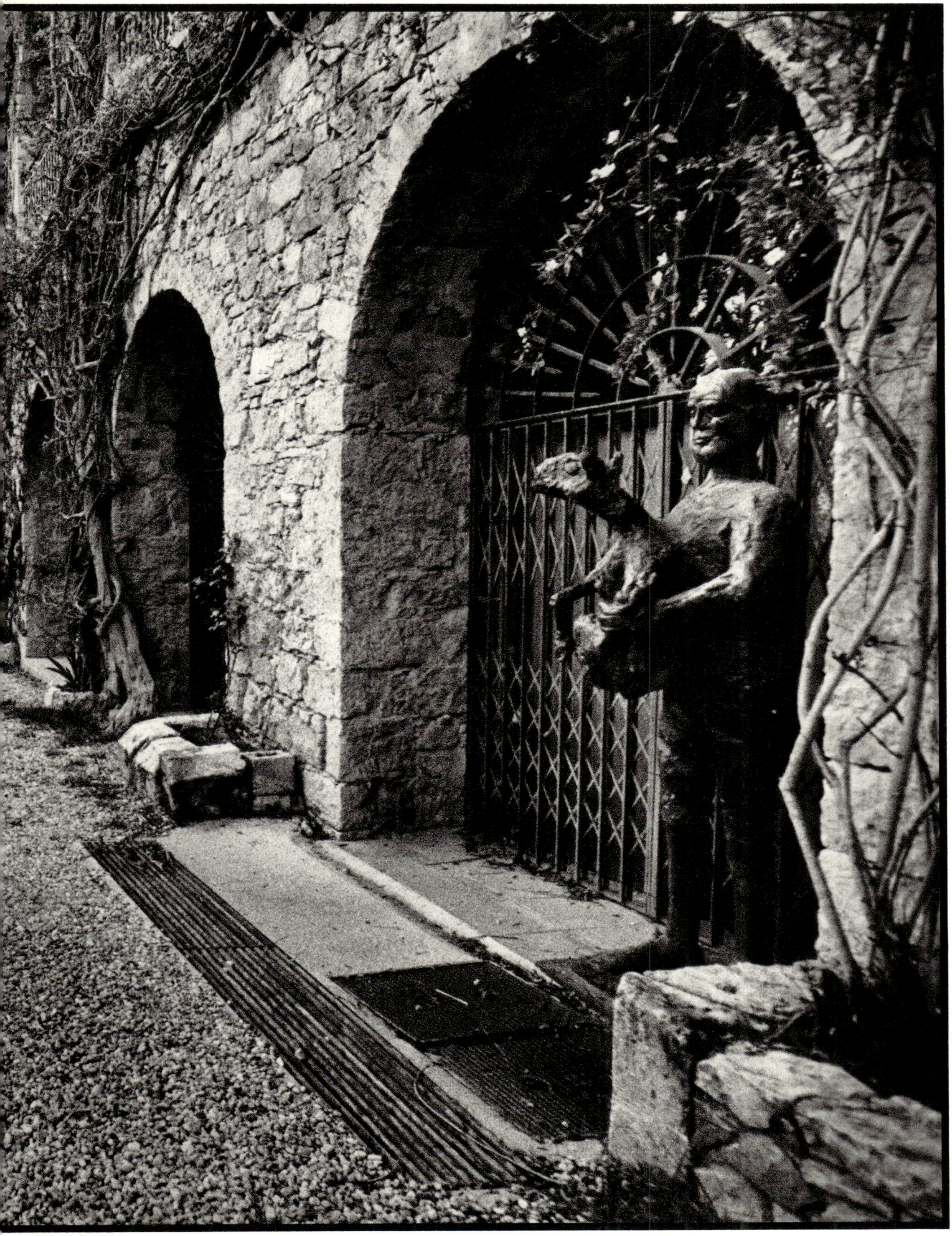

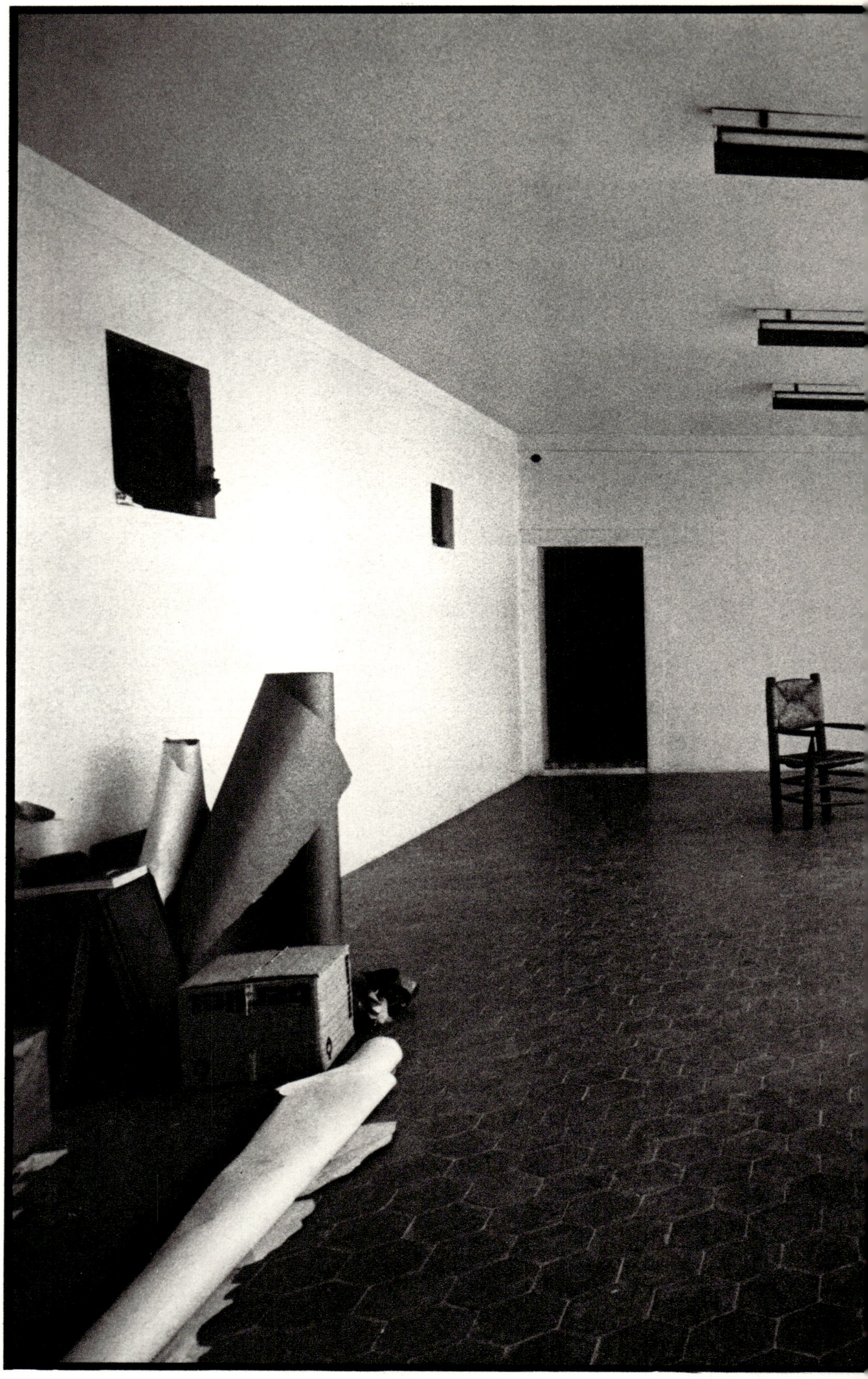

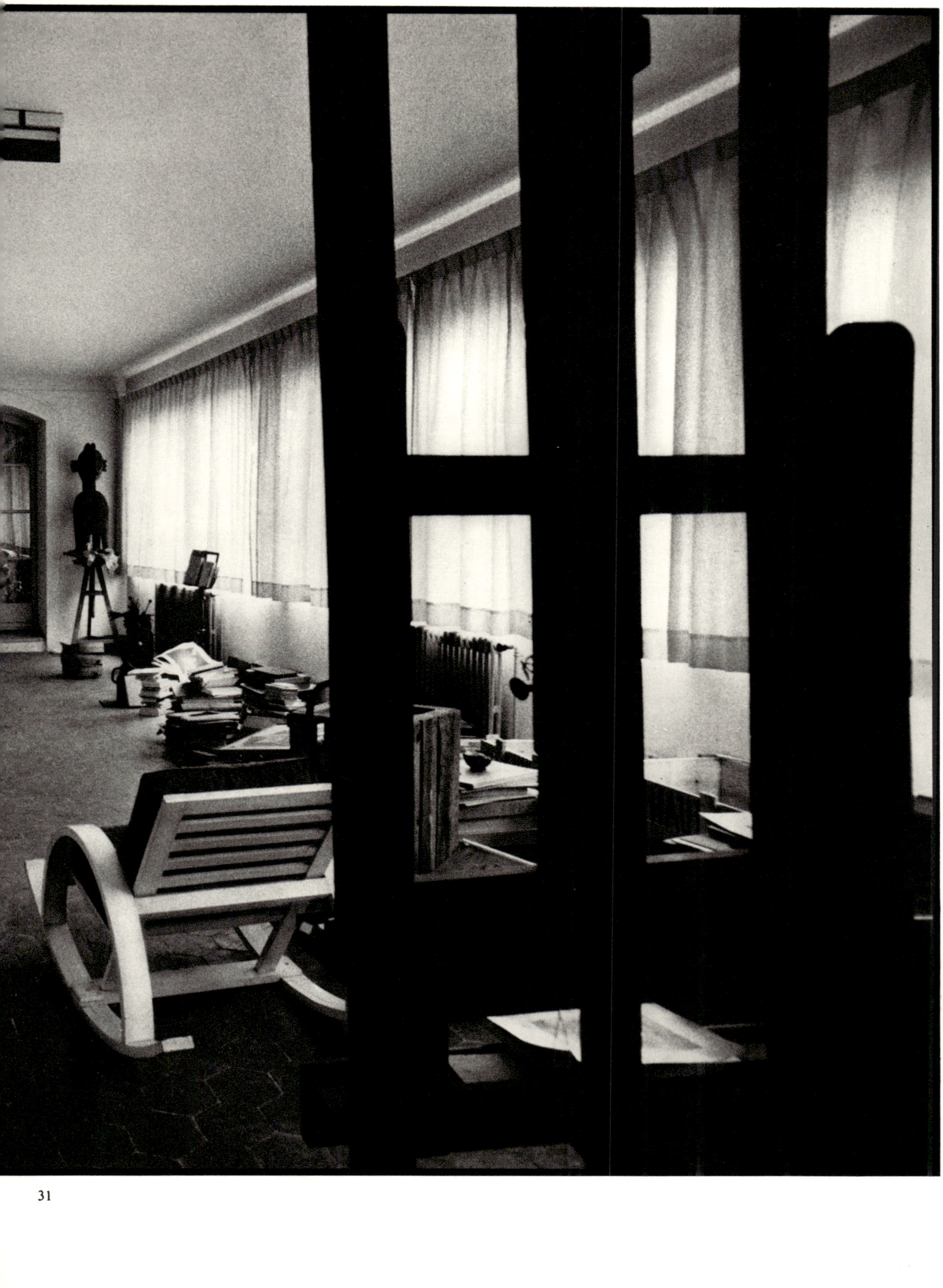

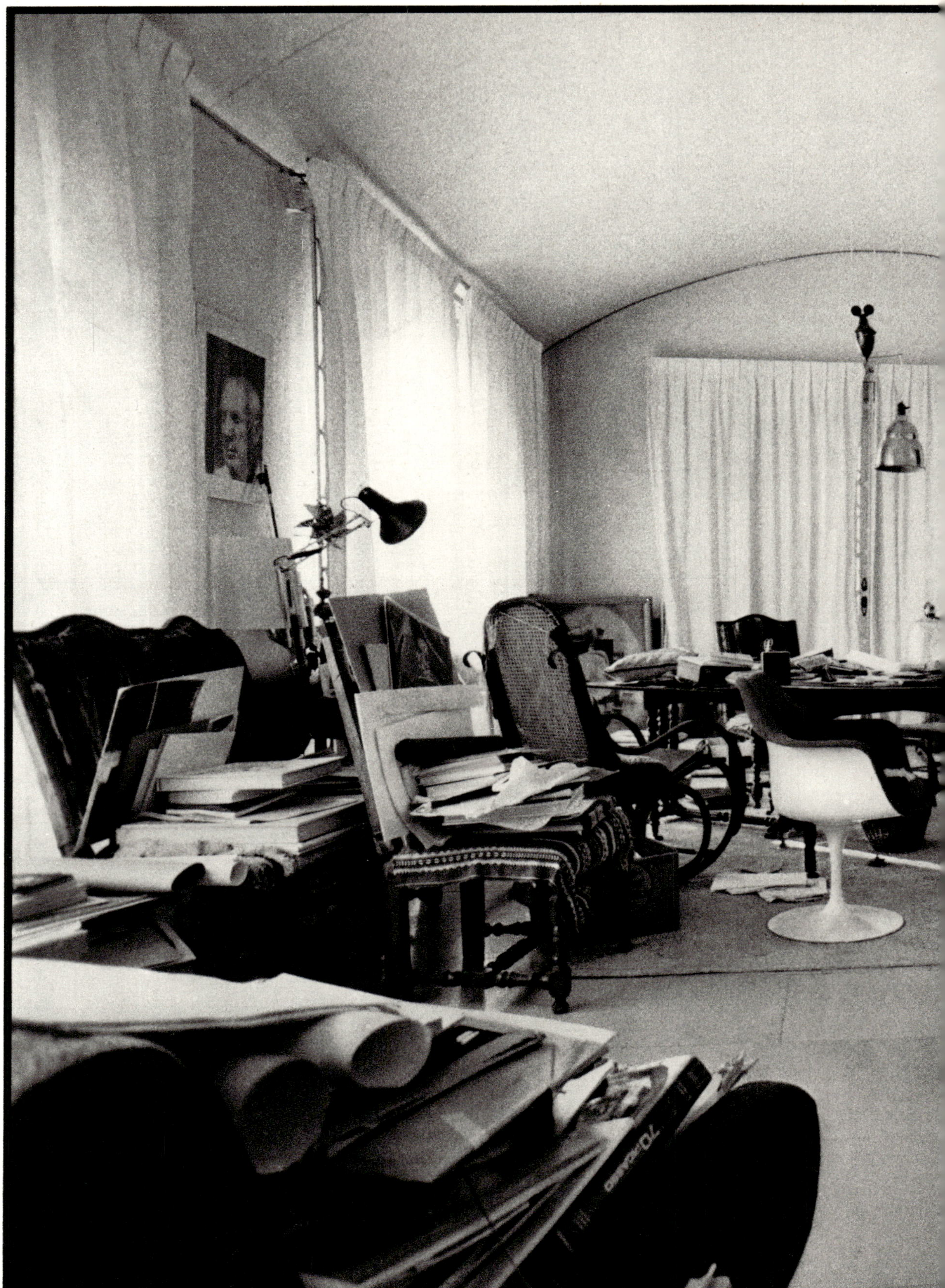

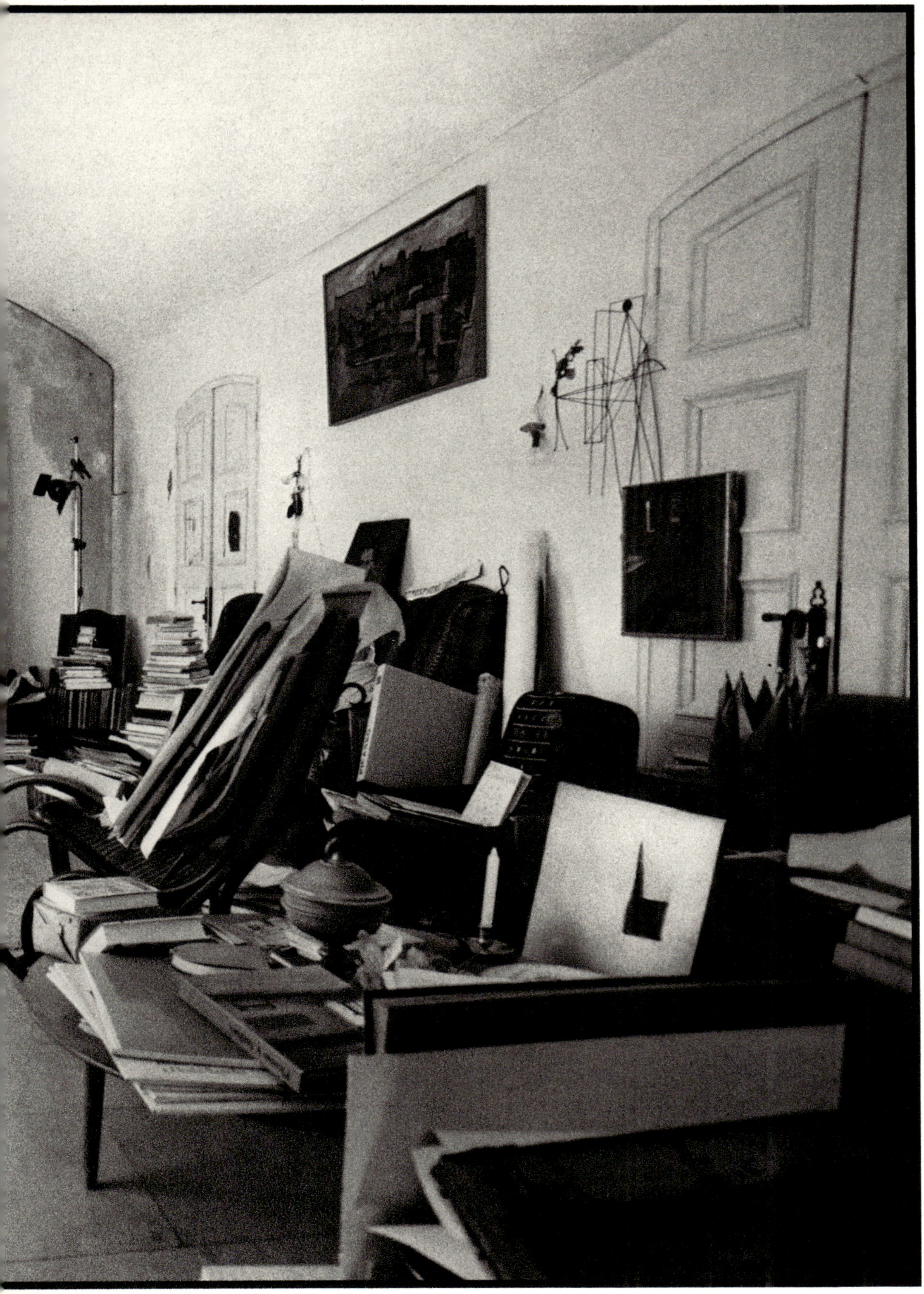

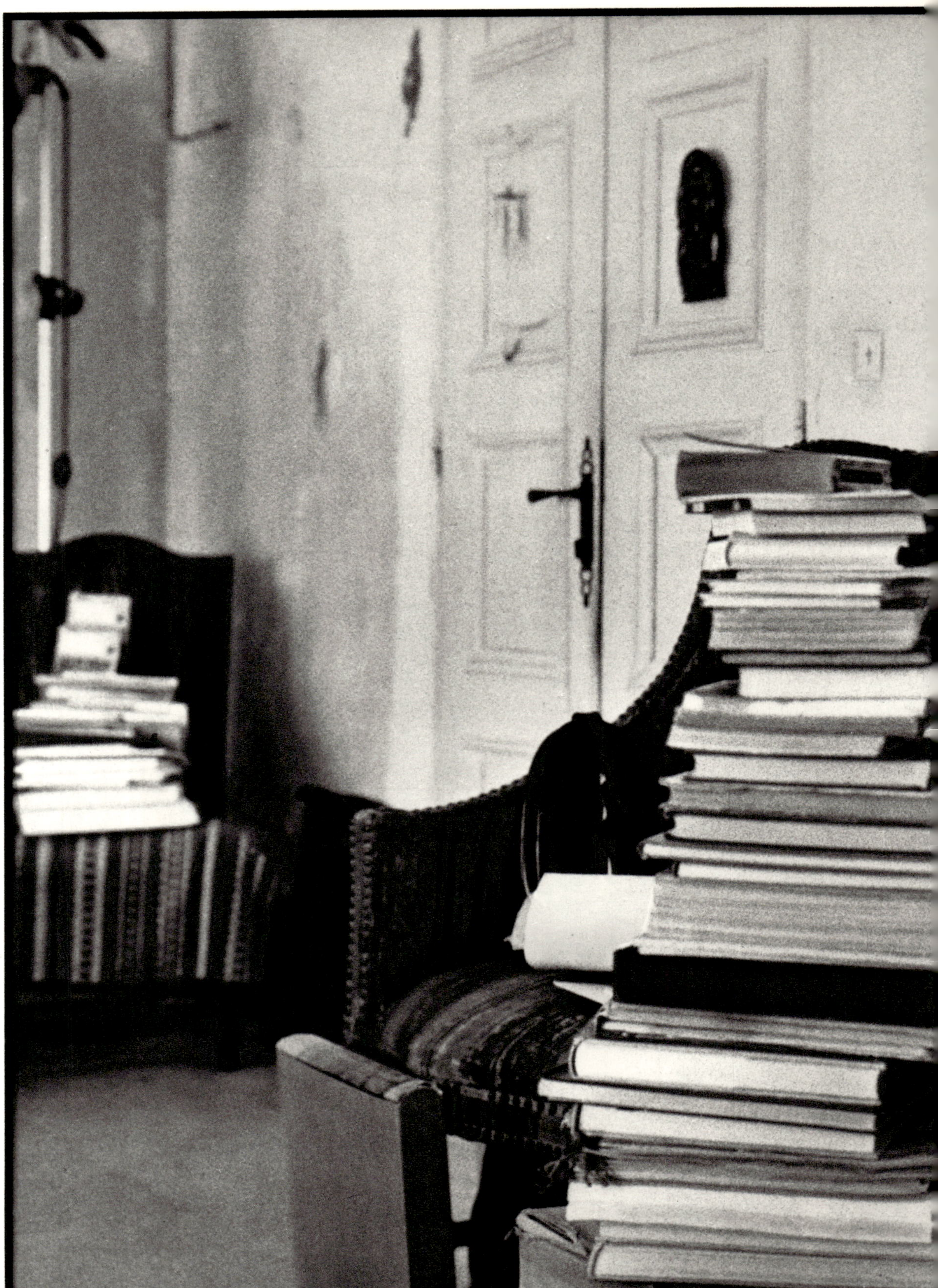

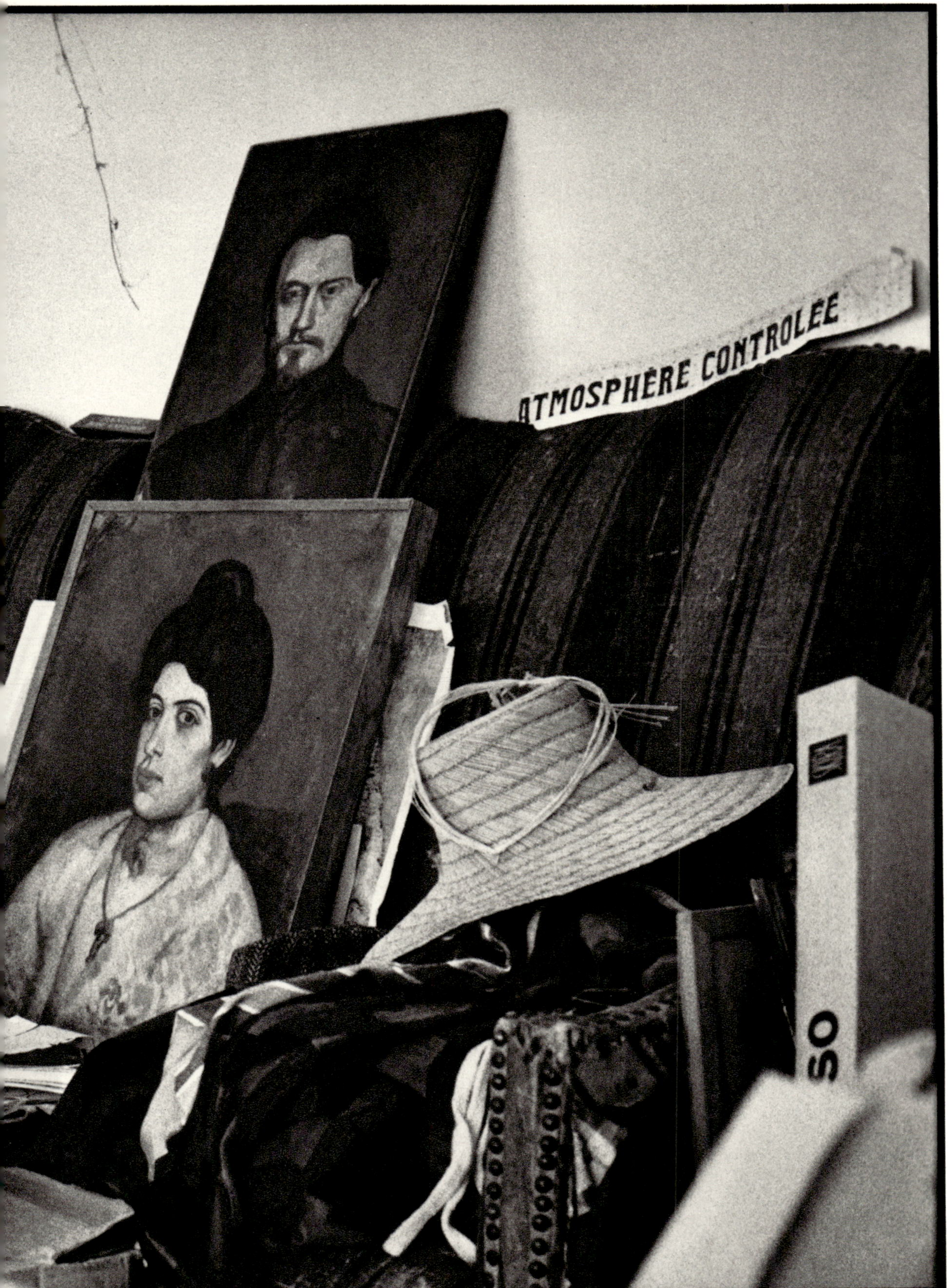
ATMOSPHÈRE CONTROLÉE

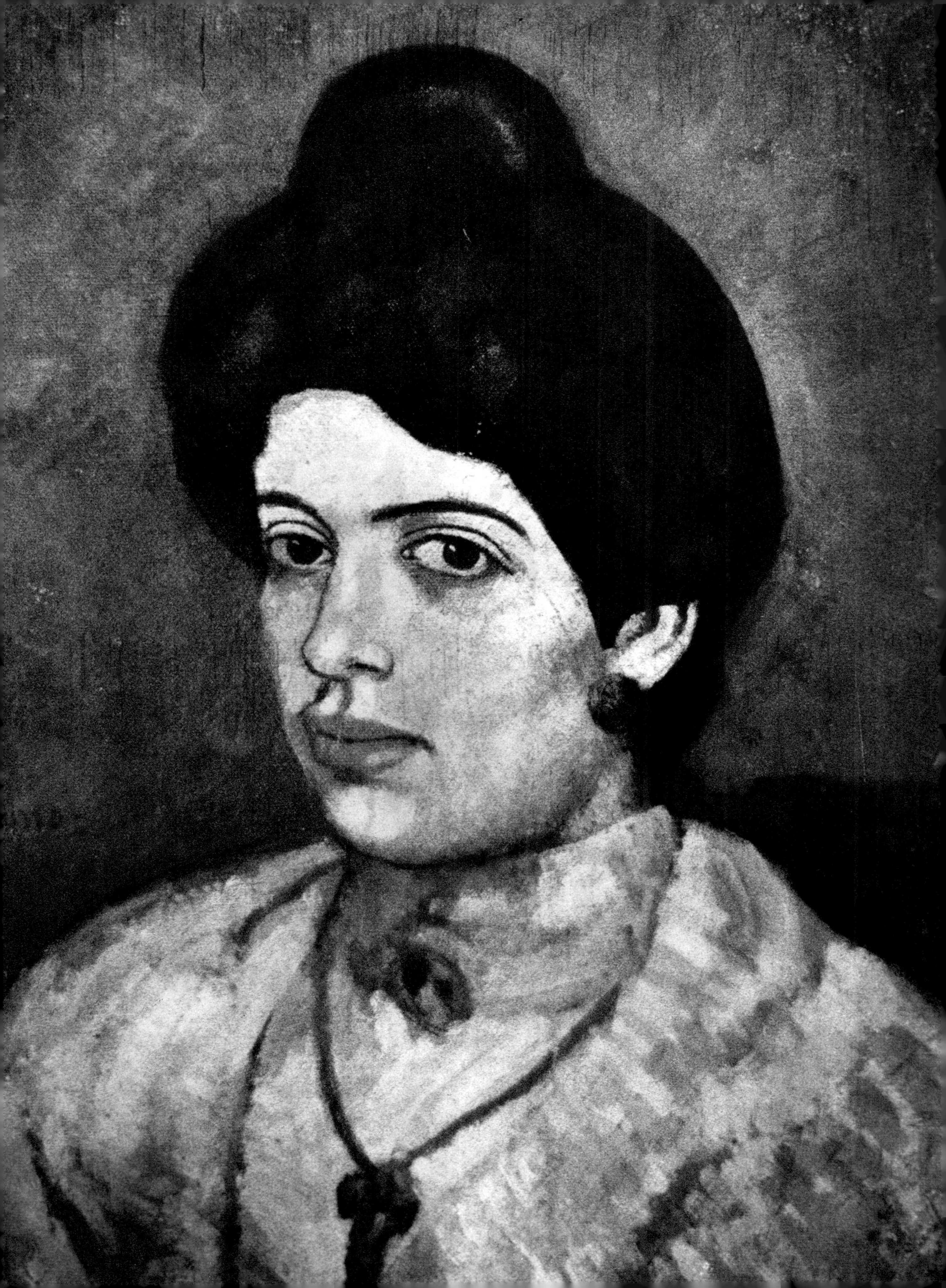

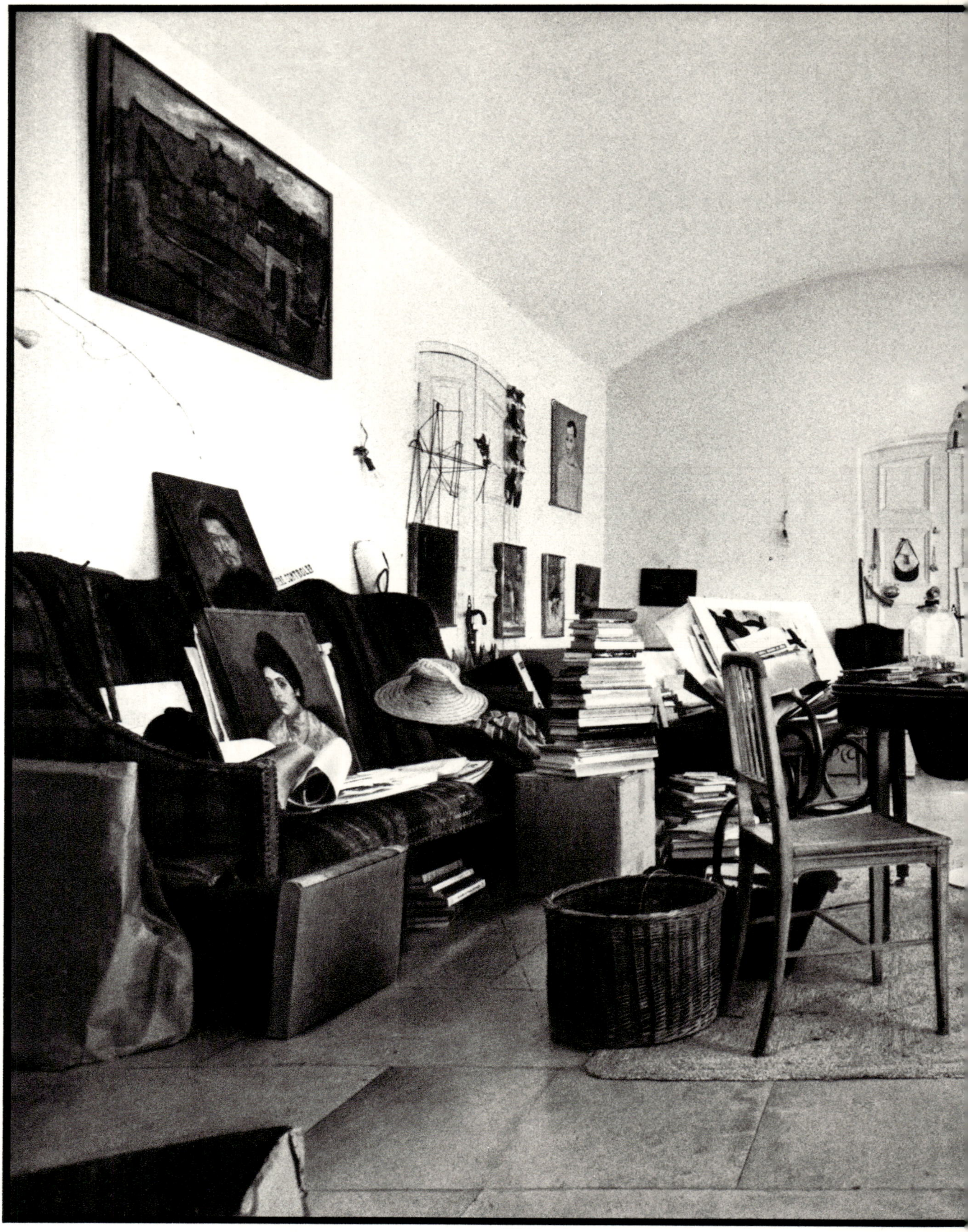

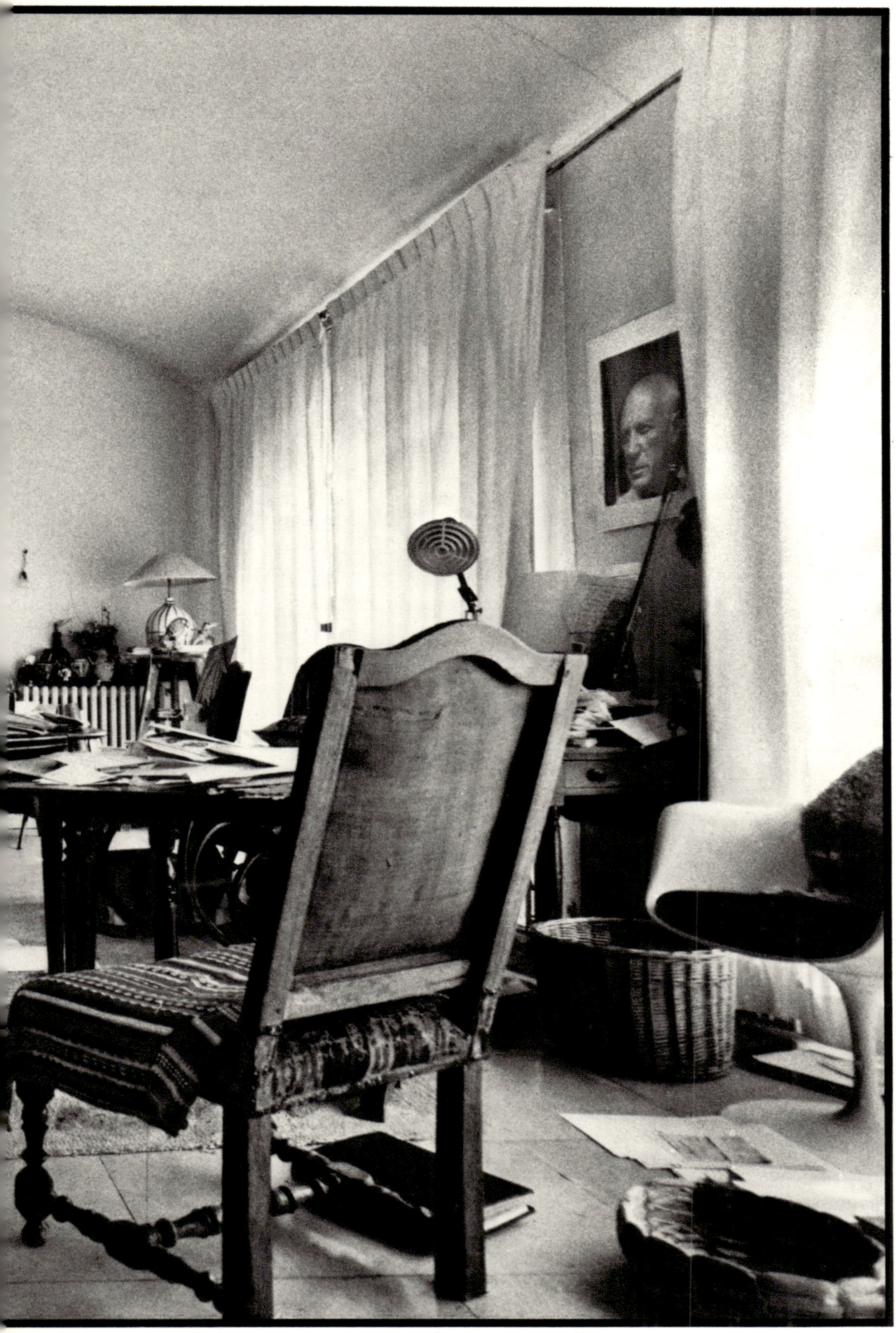

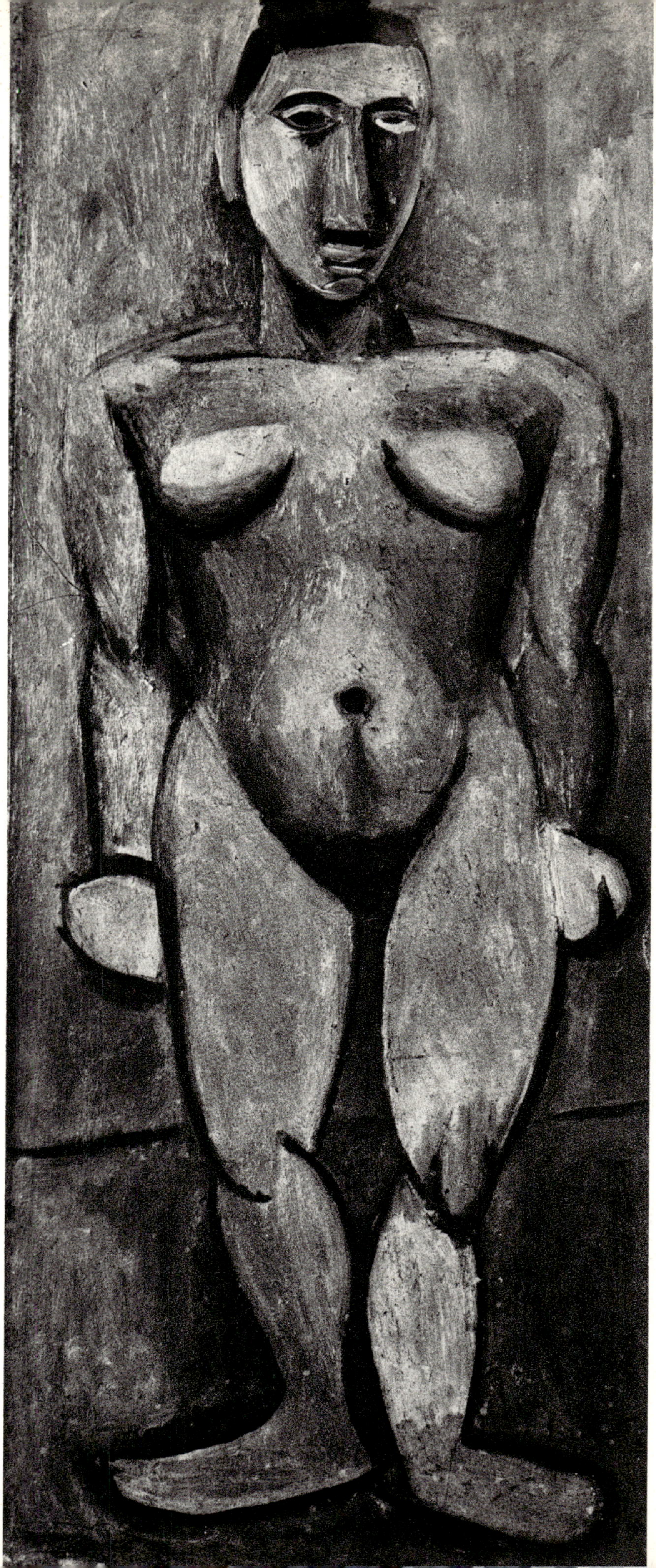

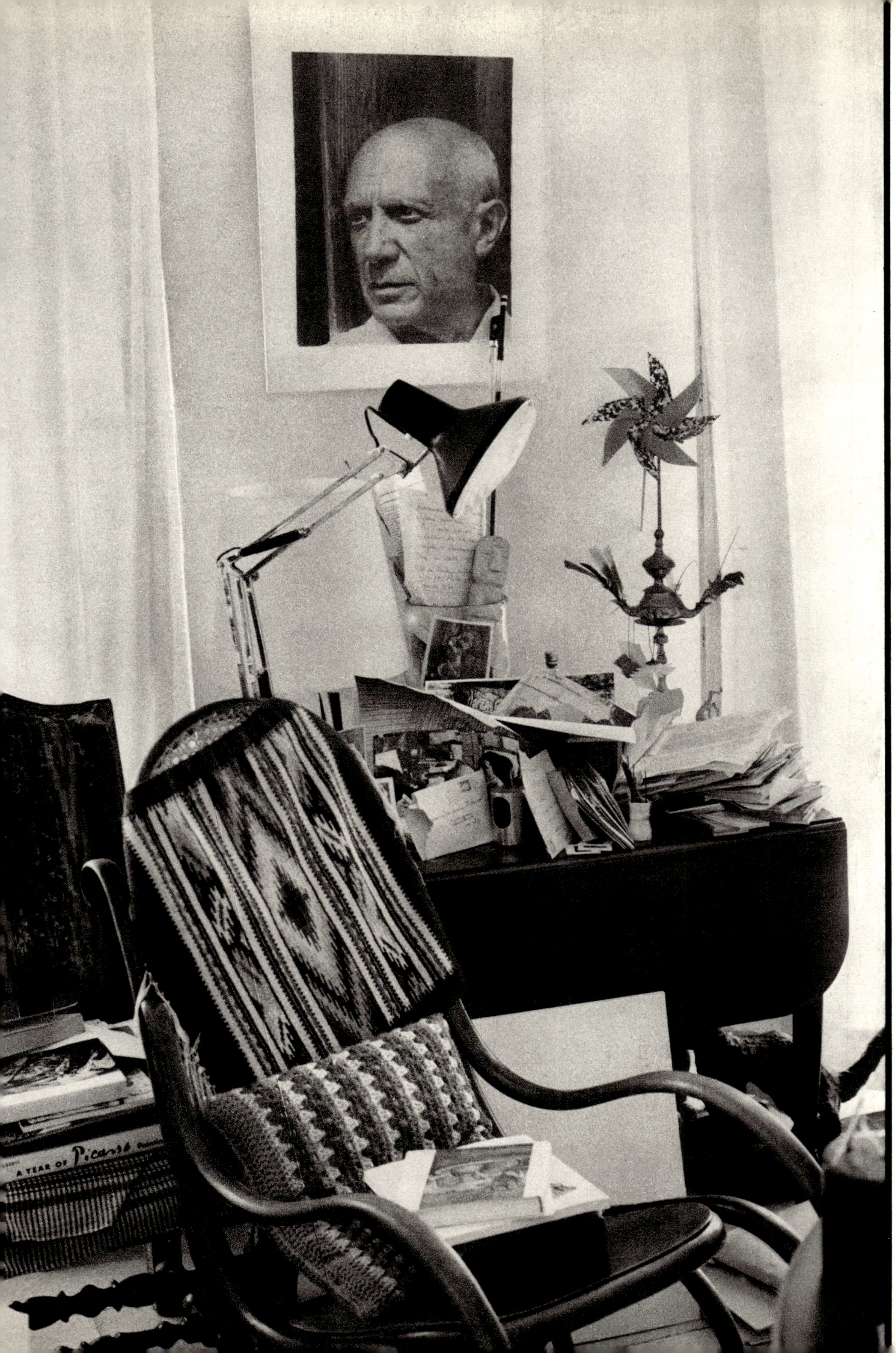
A YEAR OF Picasso

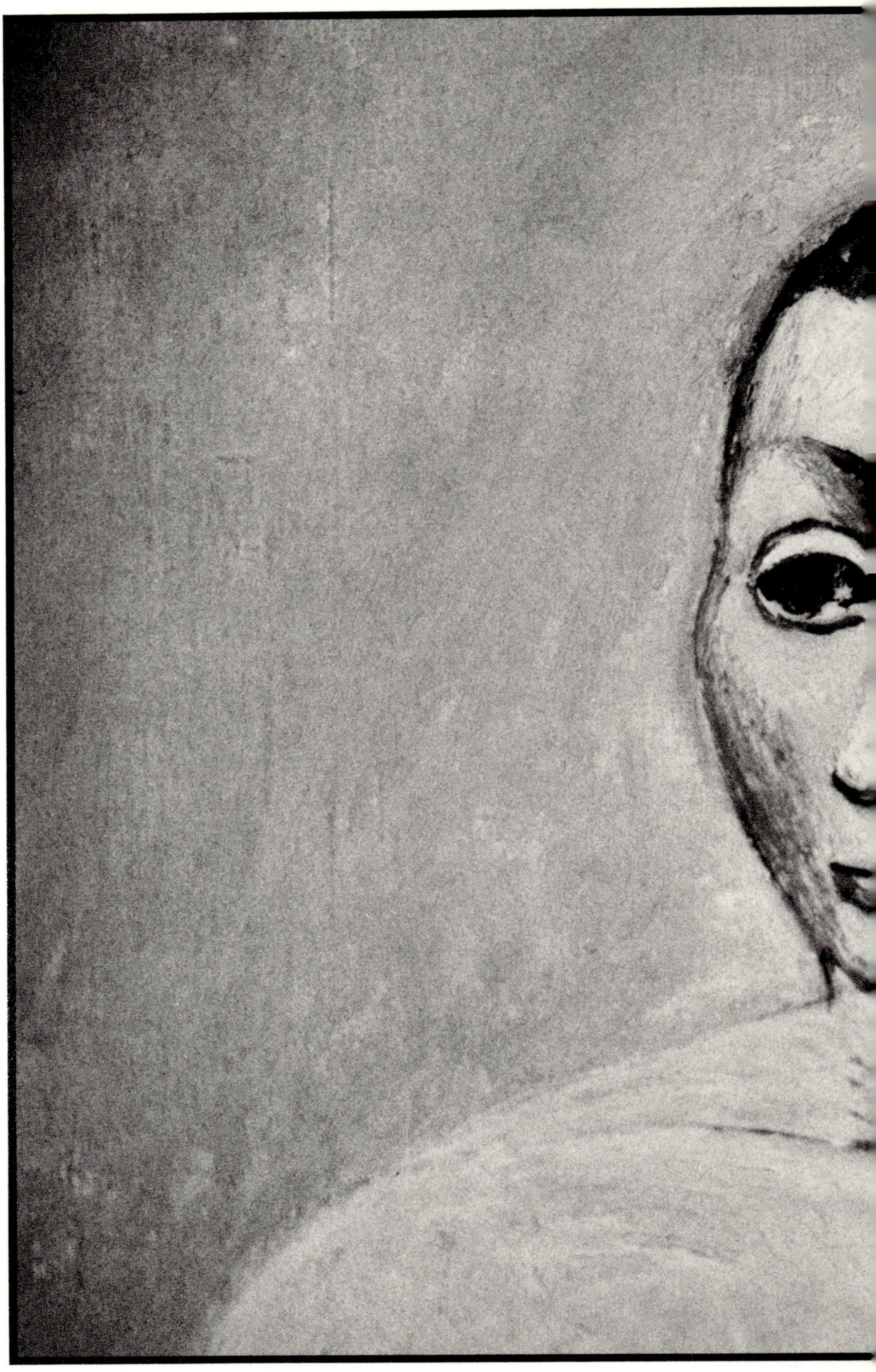

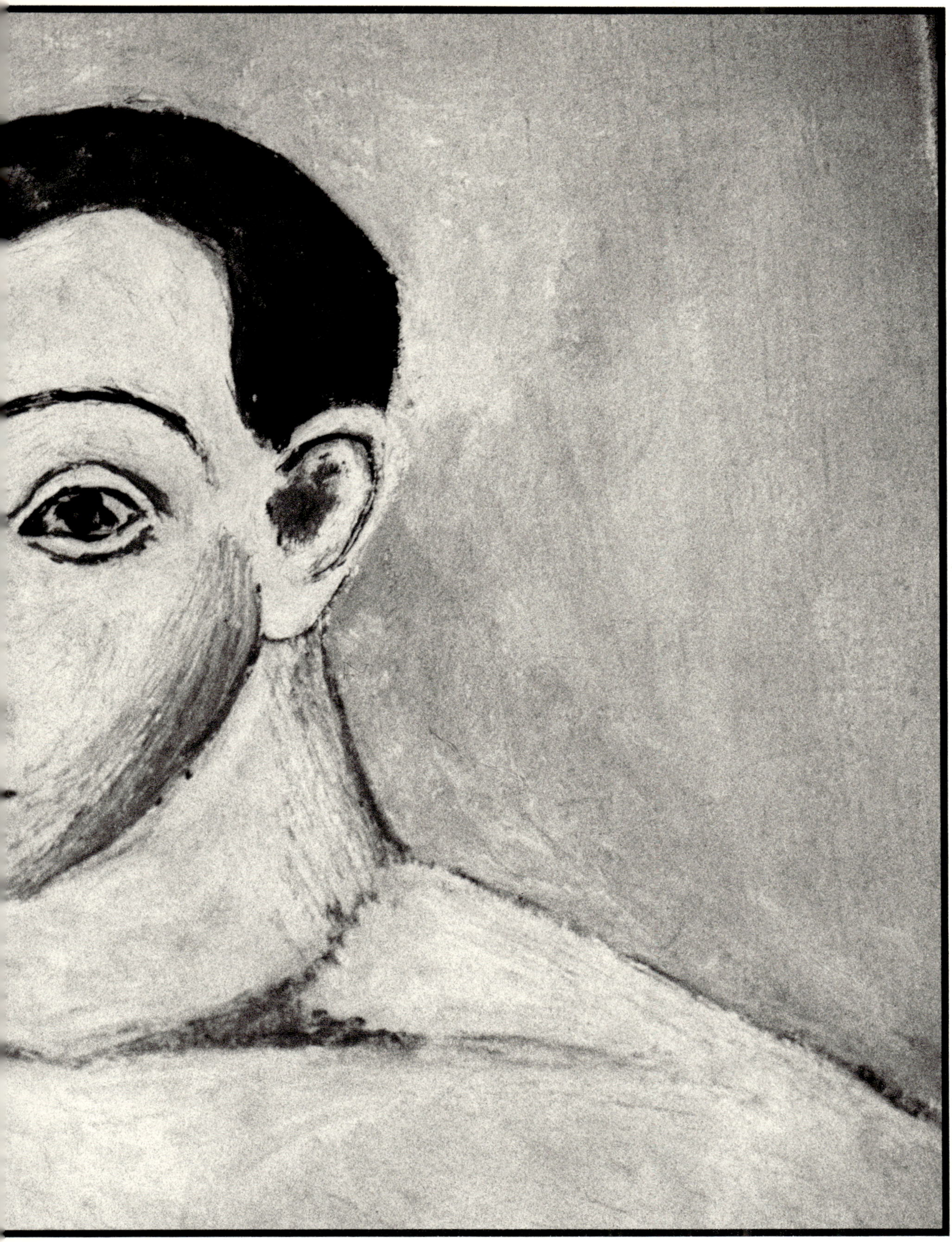

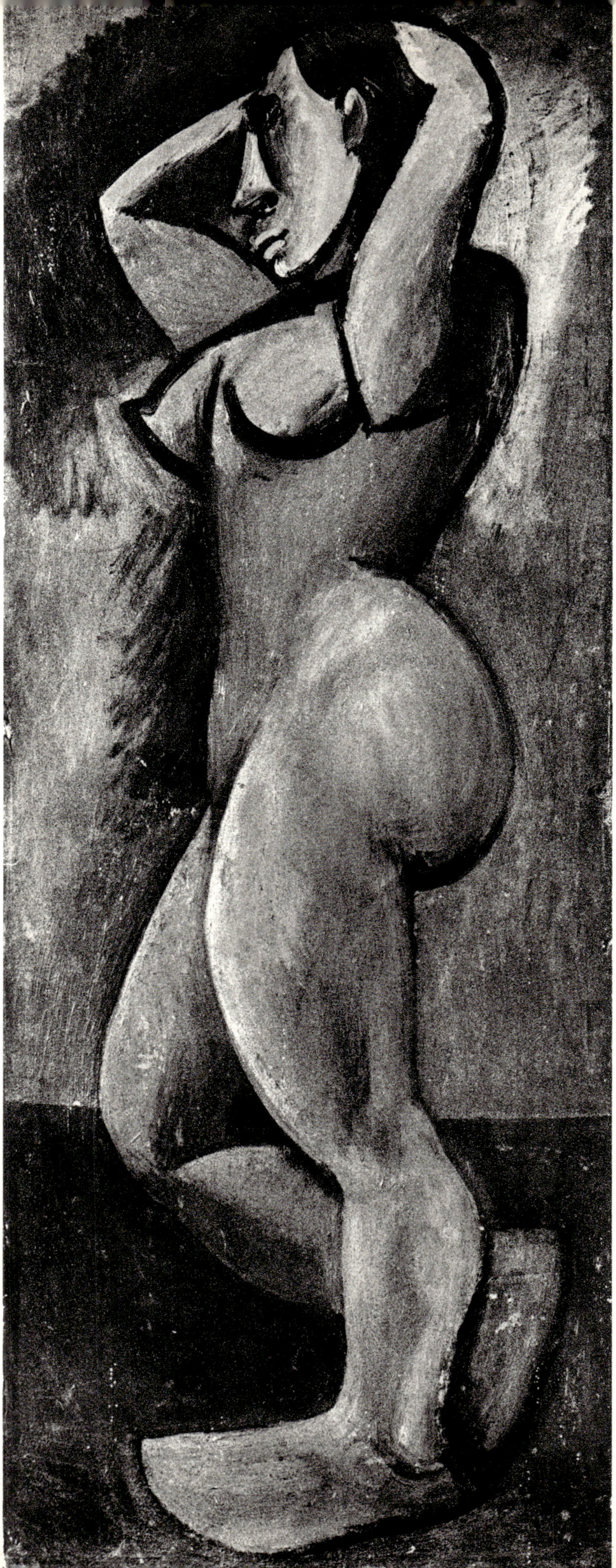

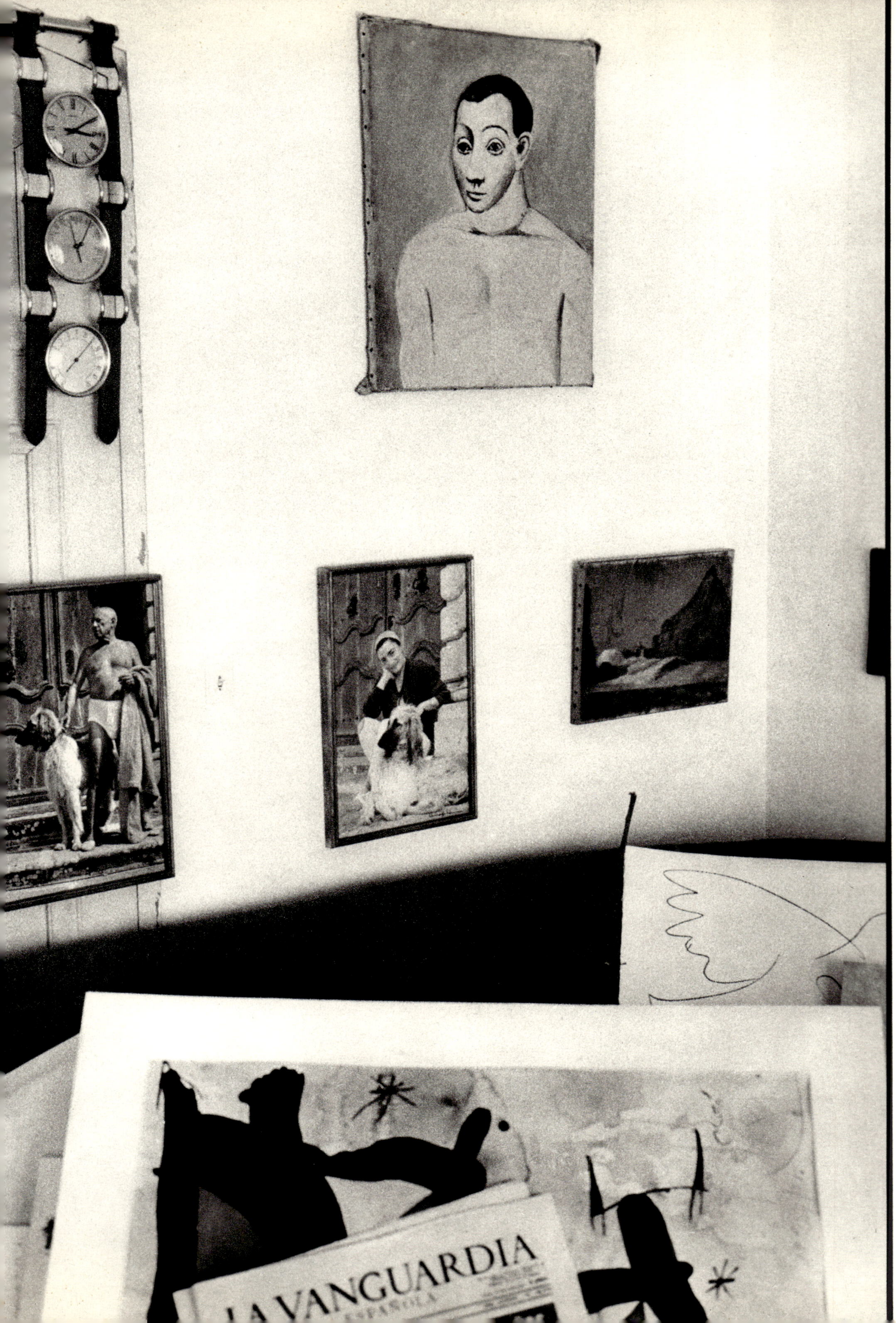
LA VANGUARDIA
ESPAÑOLA

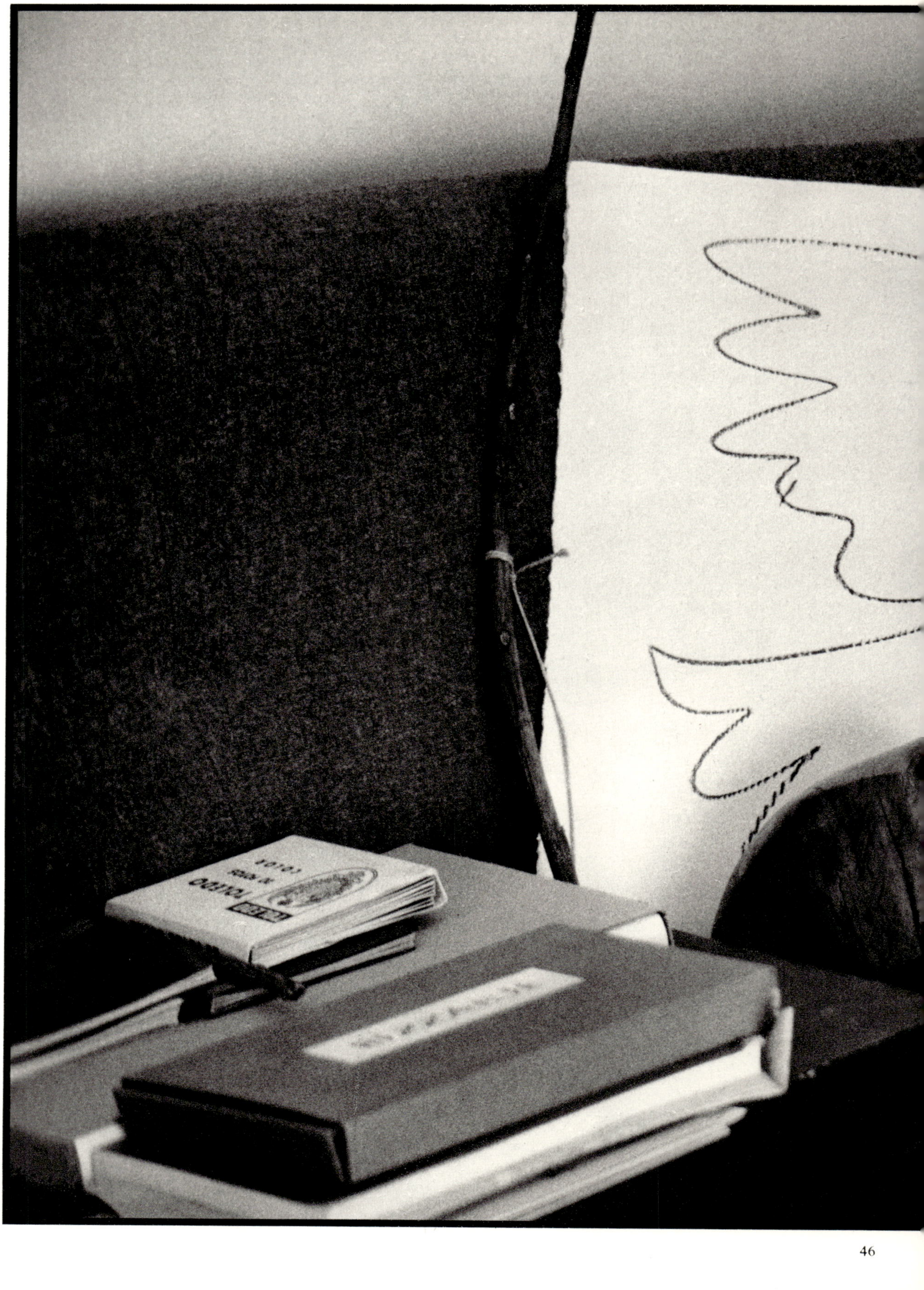

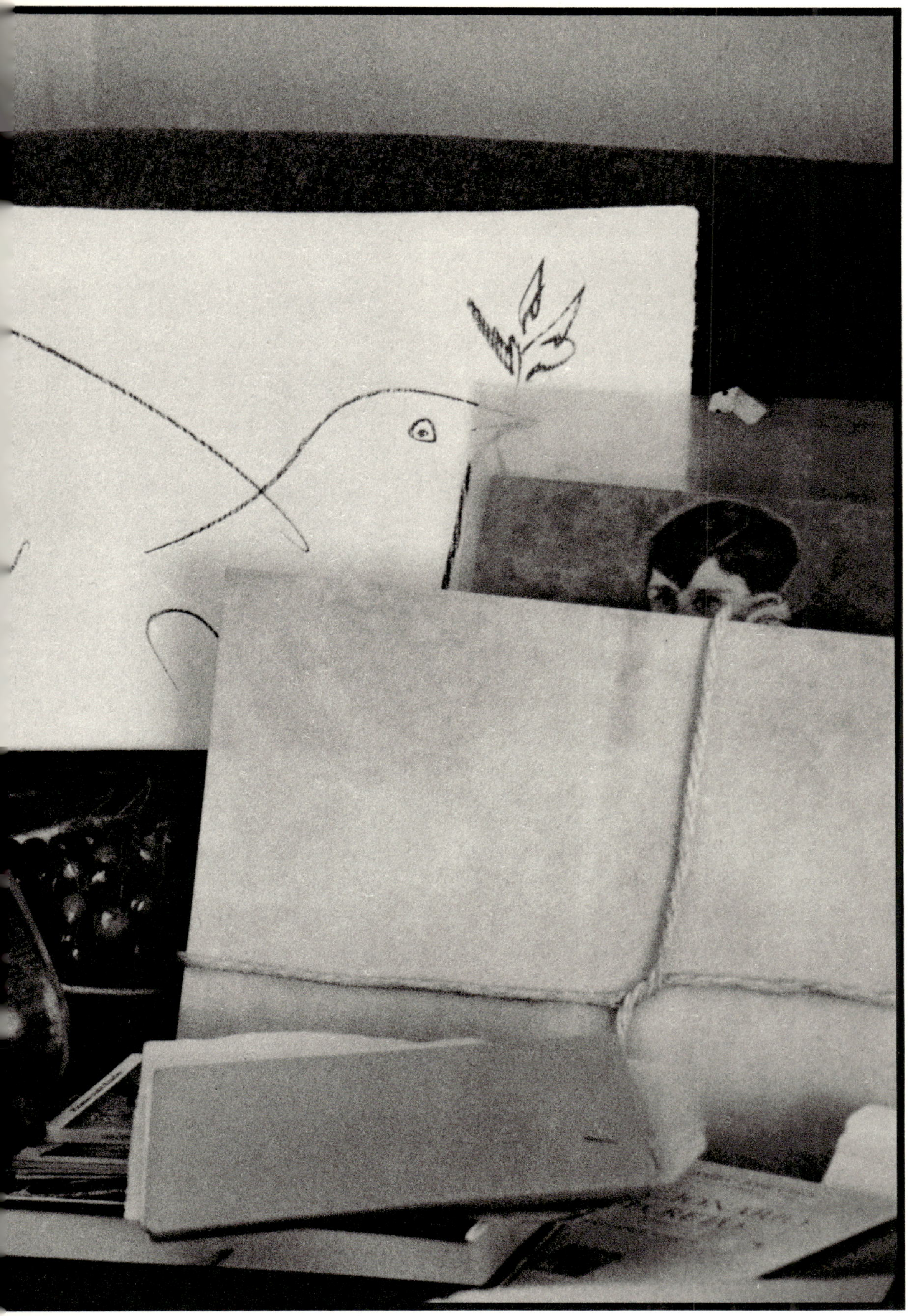

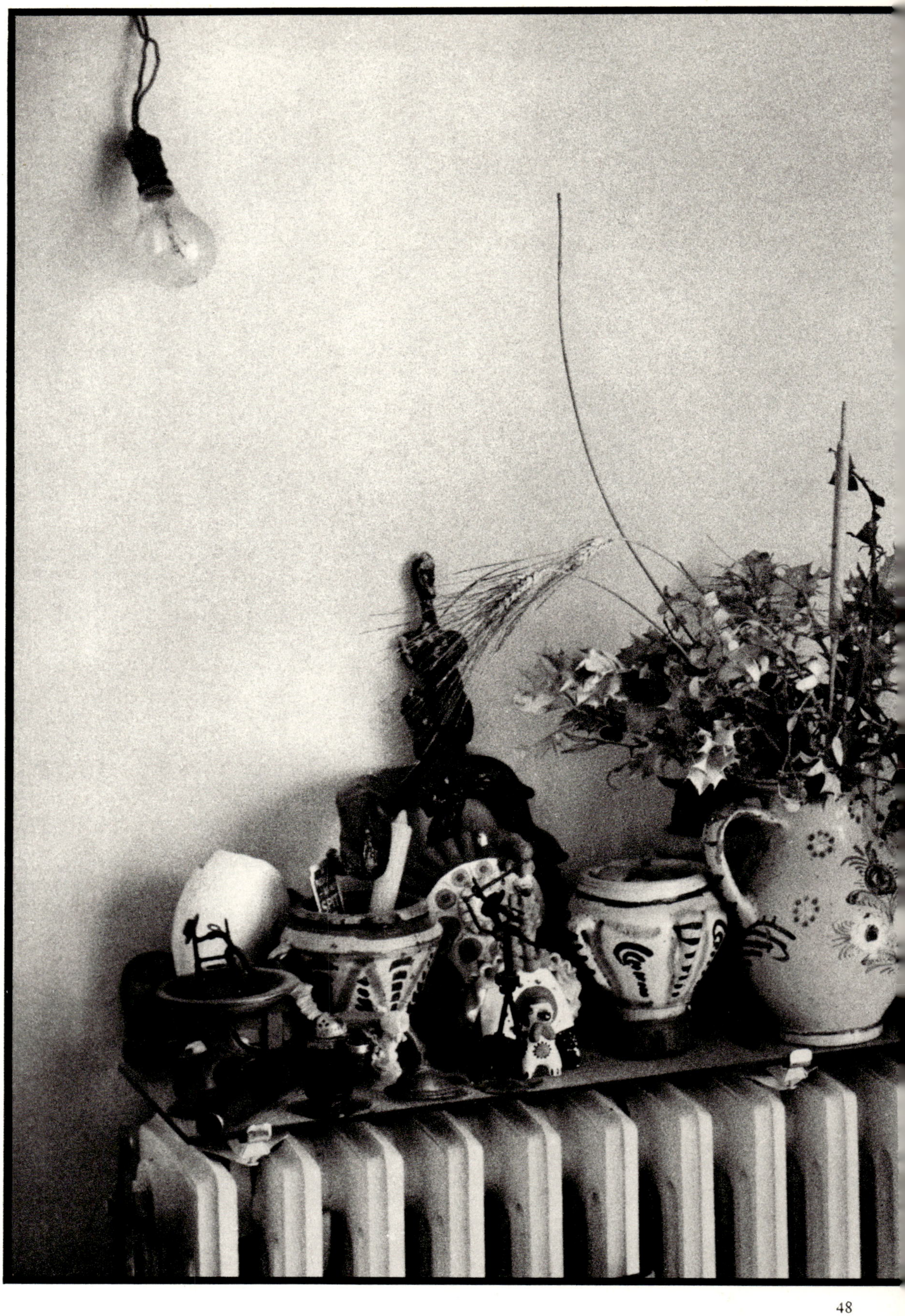

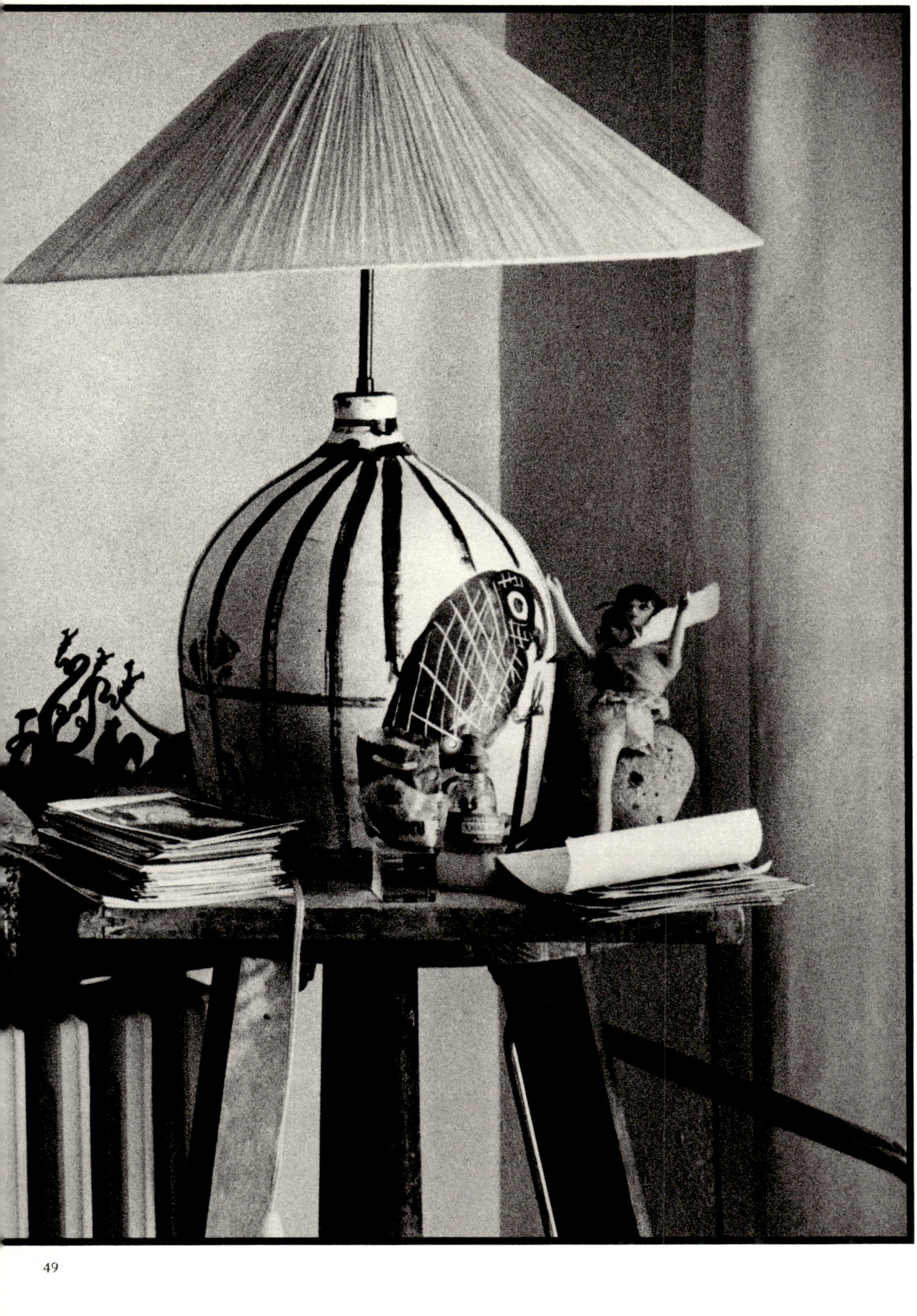

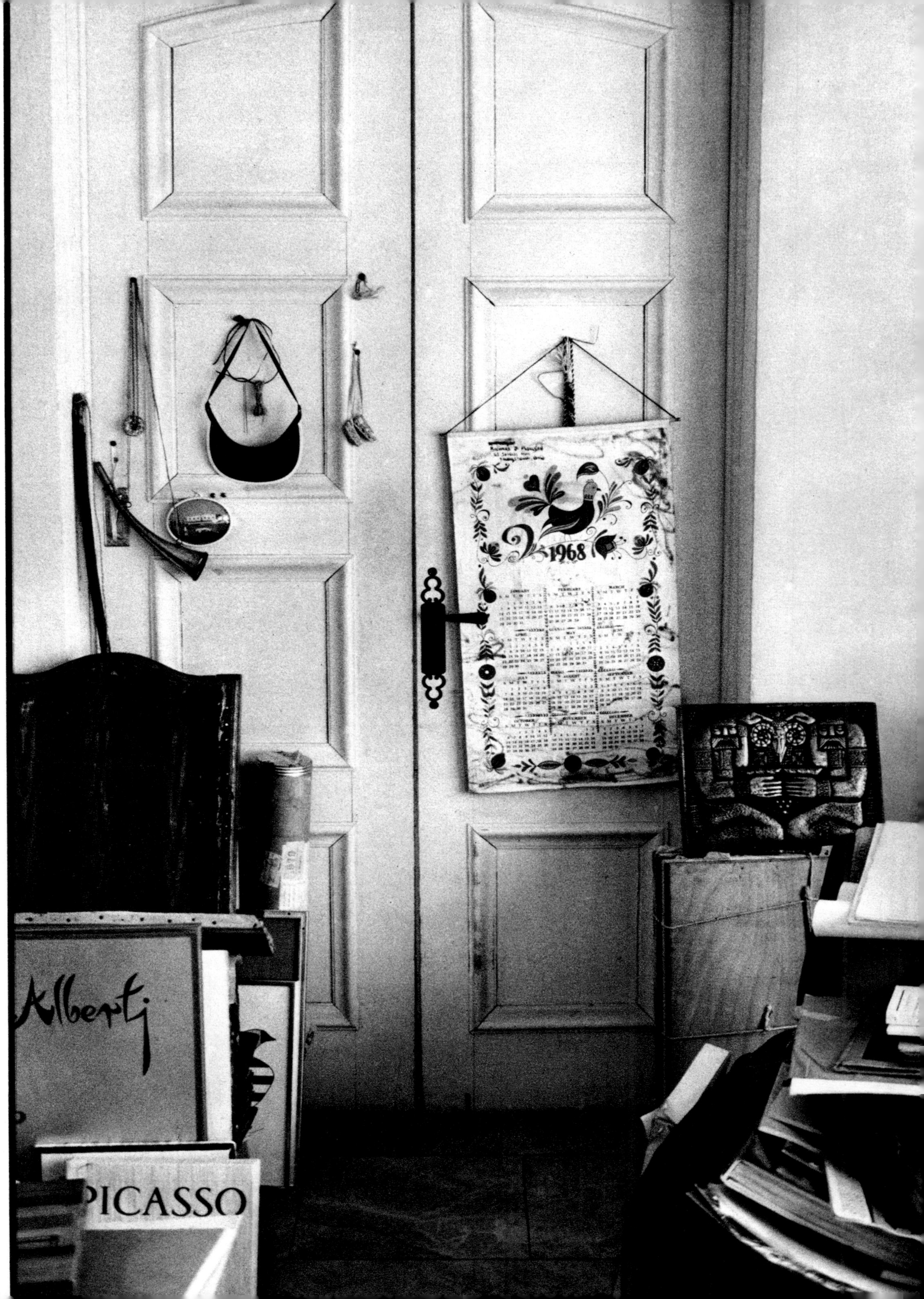
1968
Alberti
PICASSO

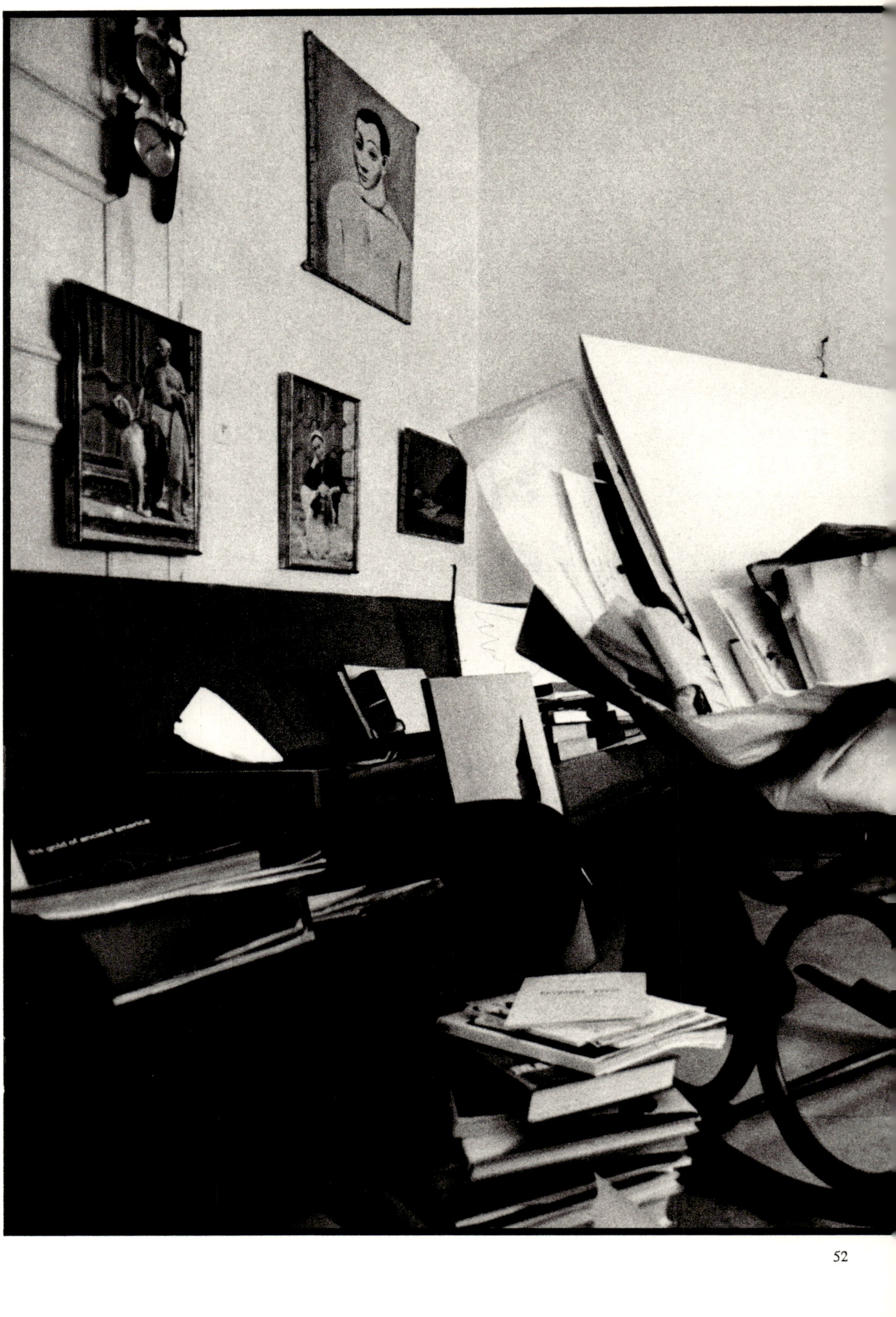

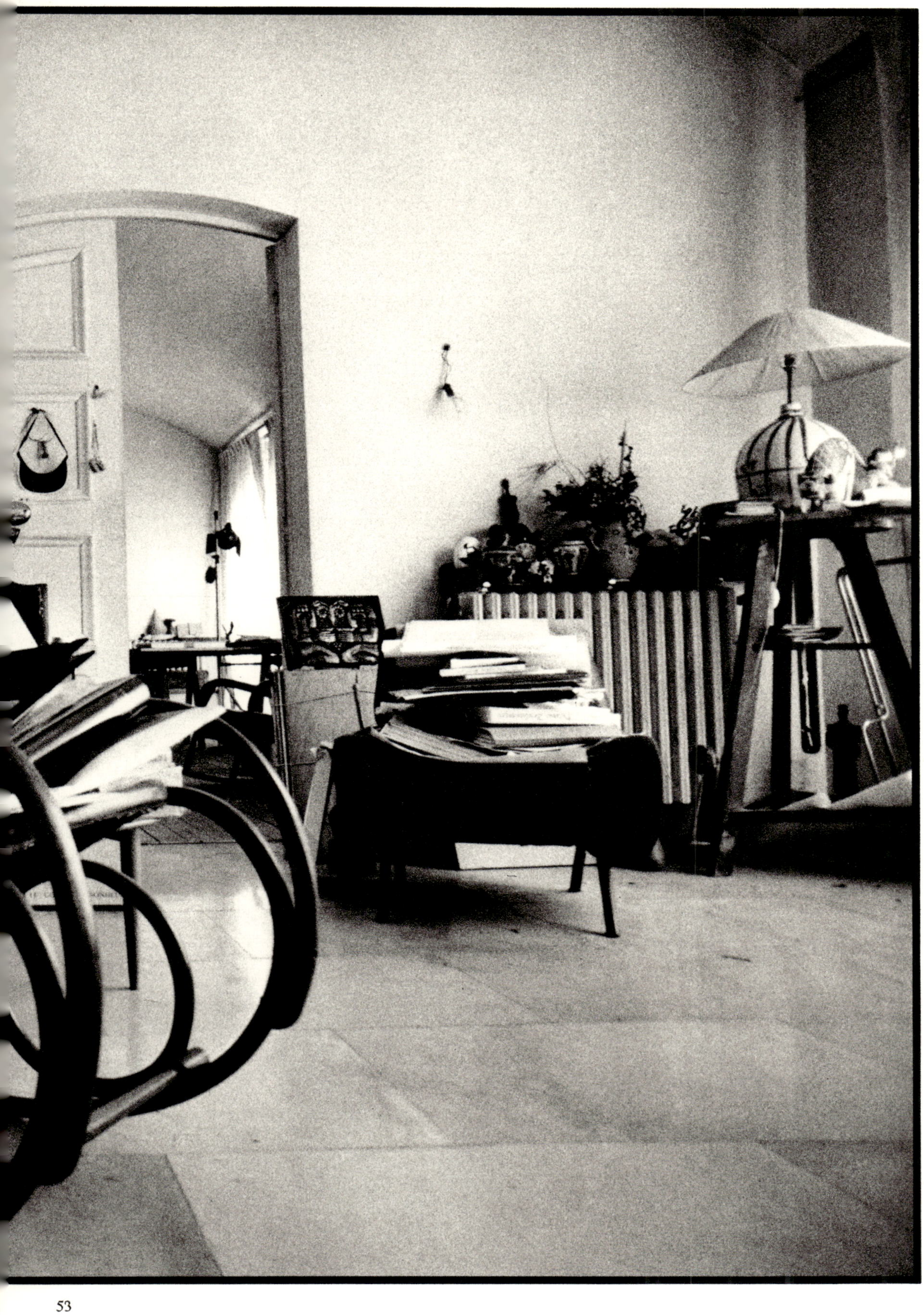

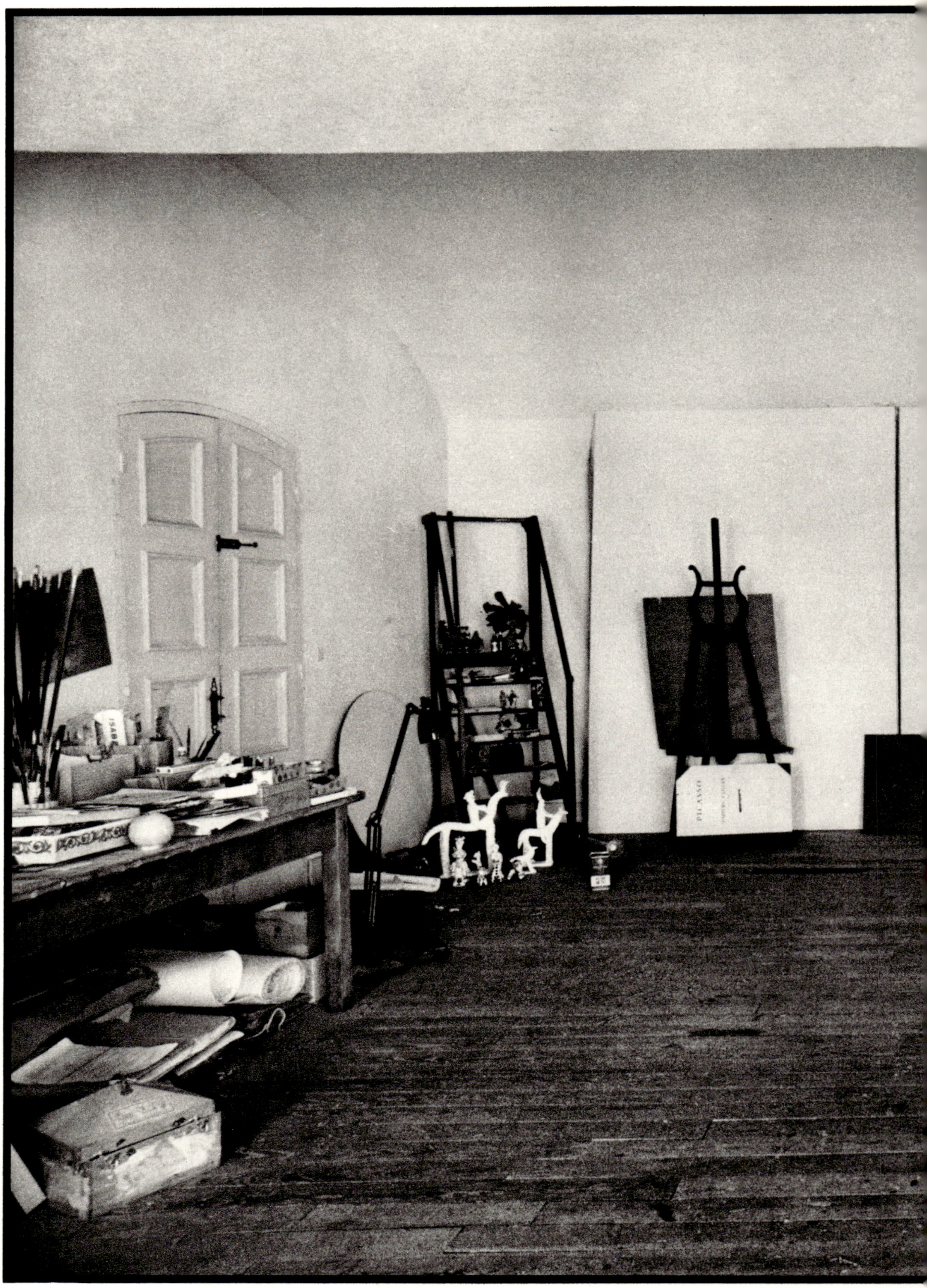

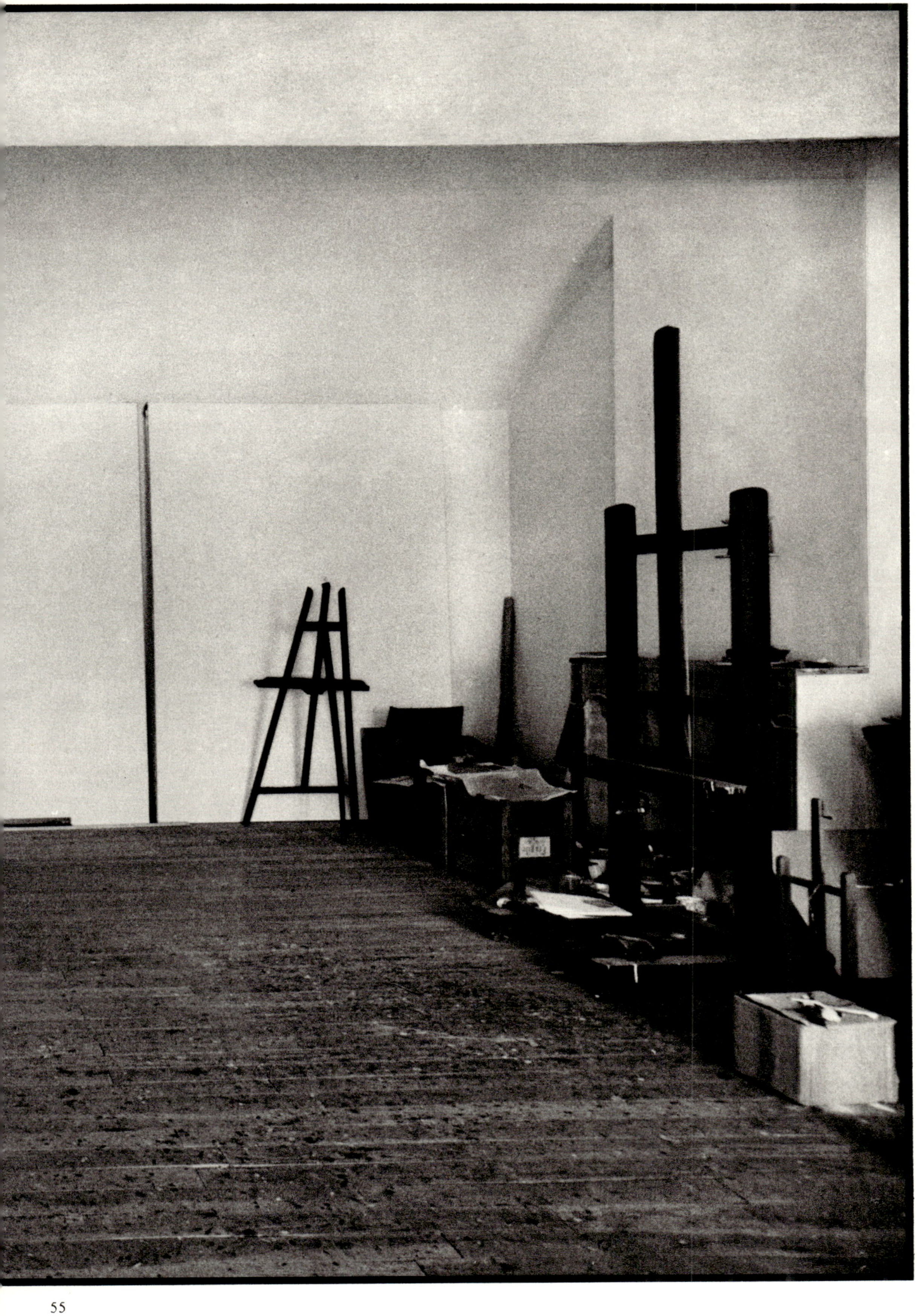

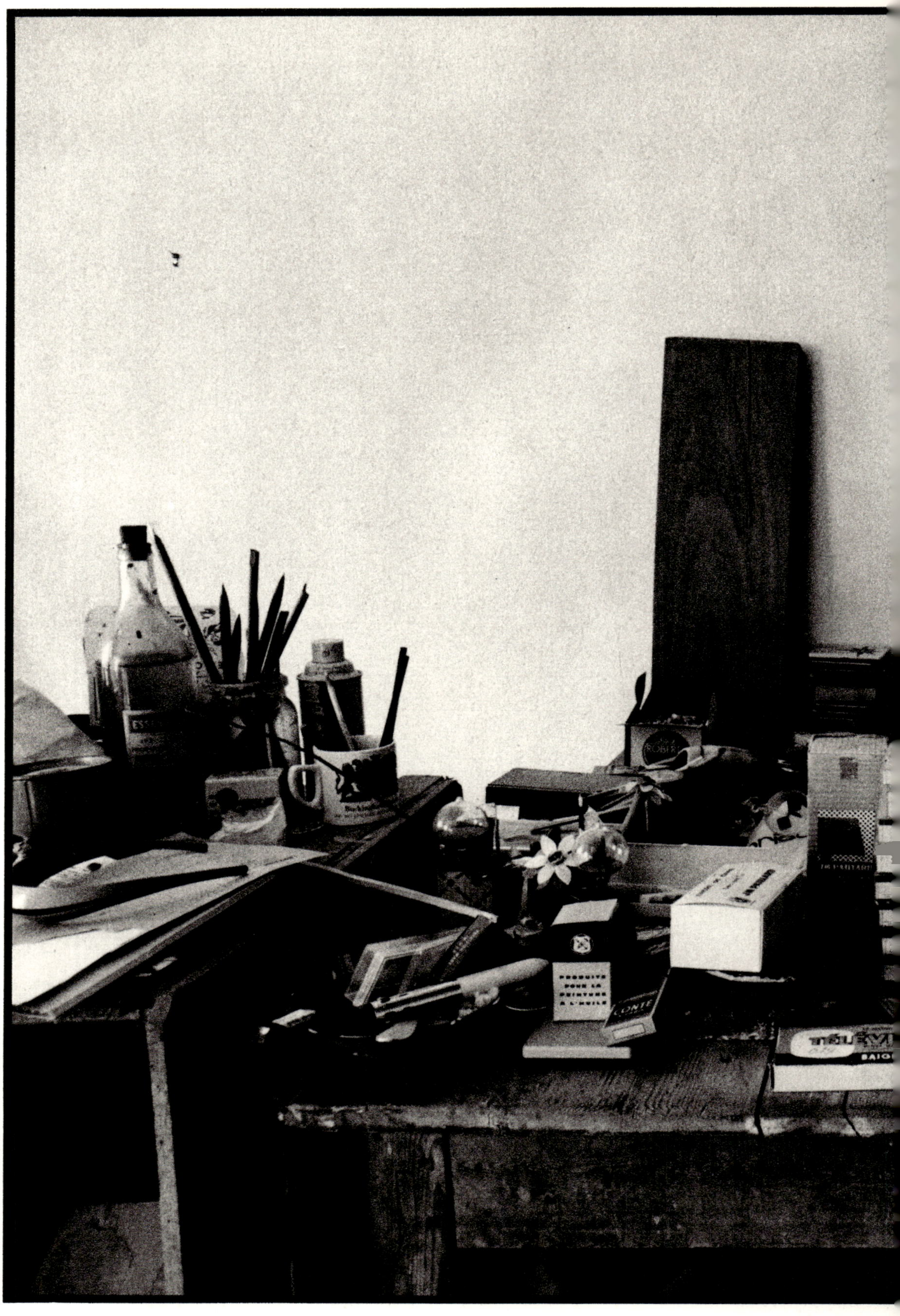
PRODUITS POUR LA PEINTURE A L'HUILE
CONTE

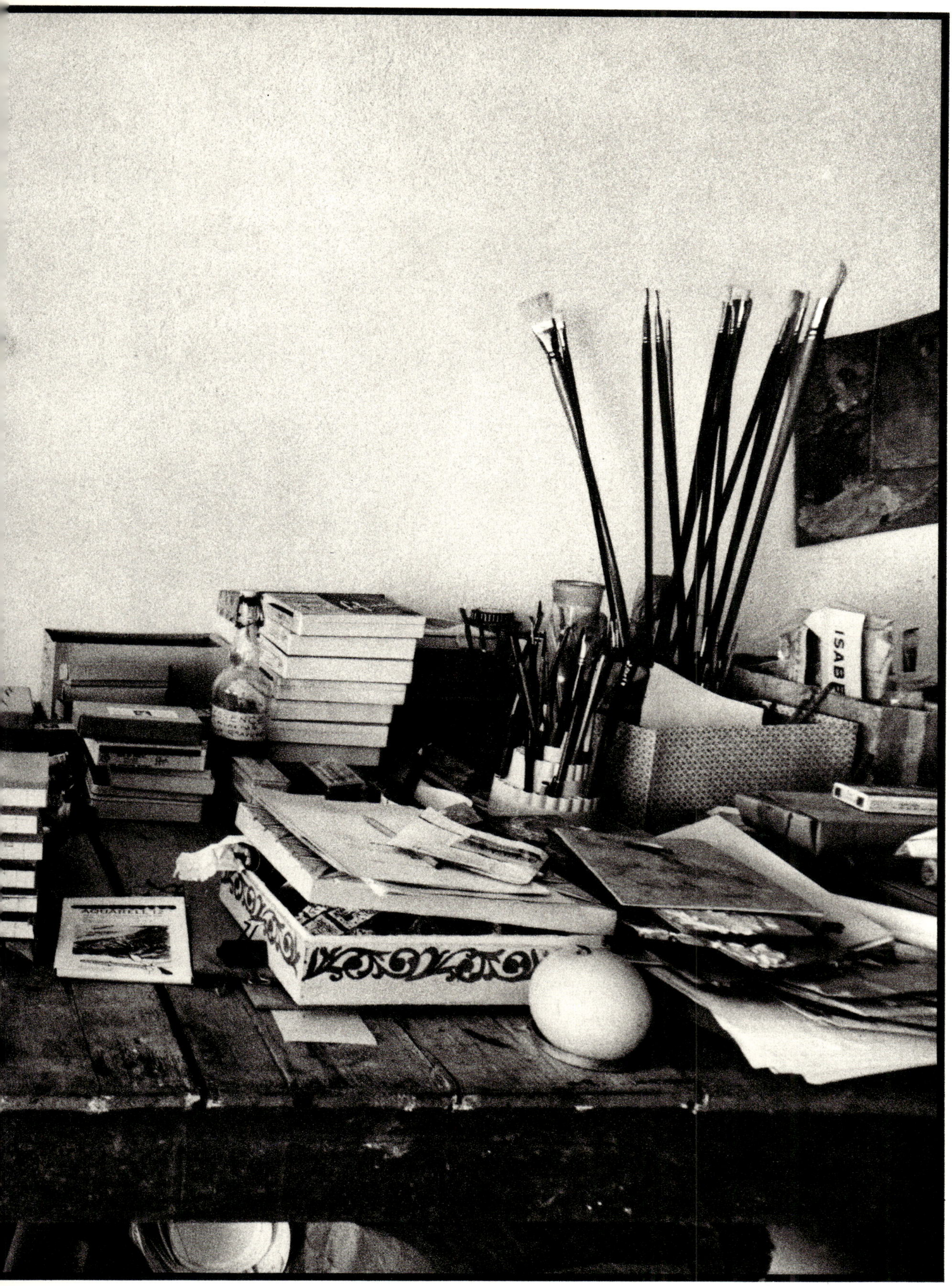
ISABE

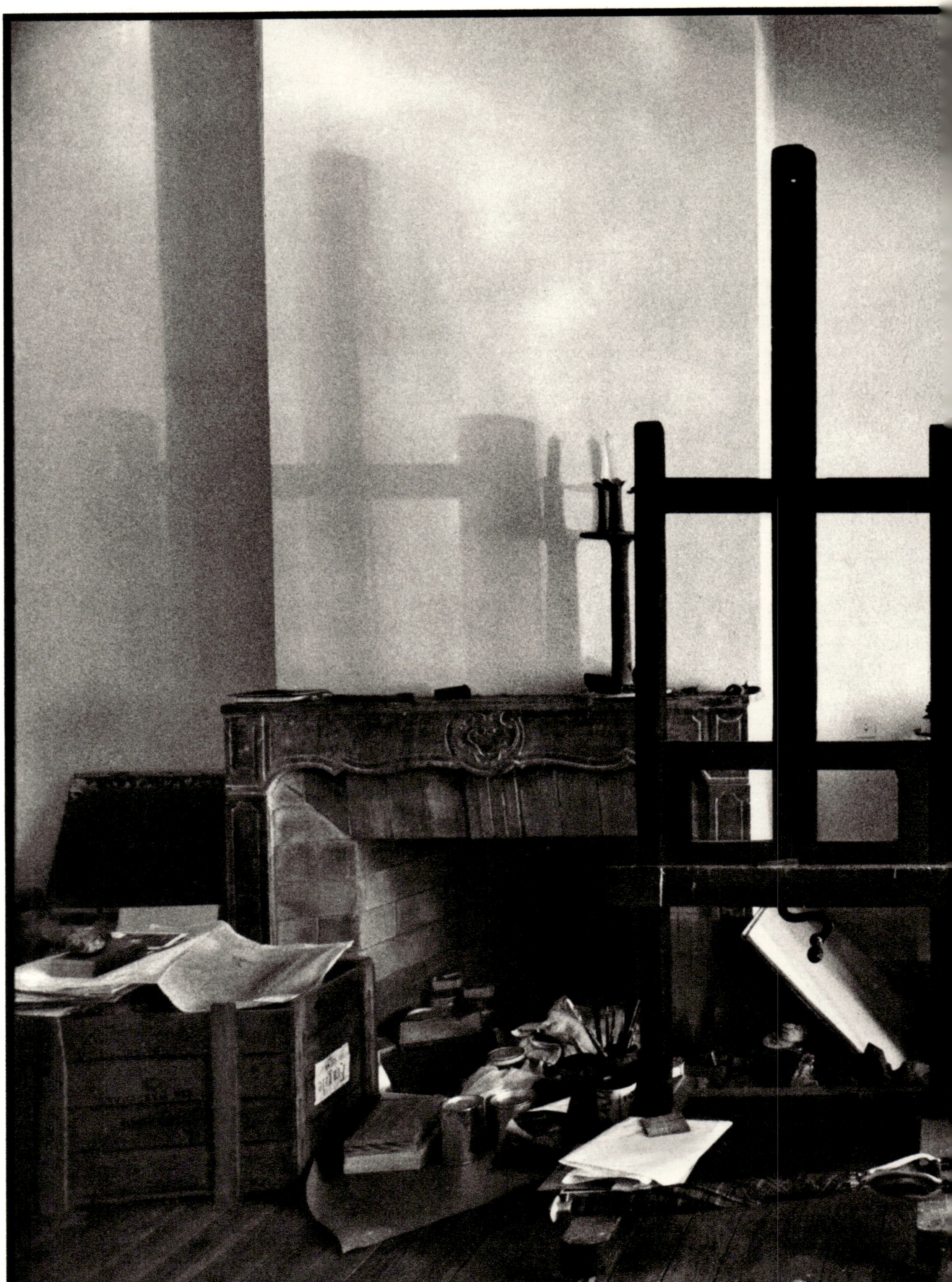

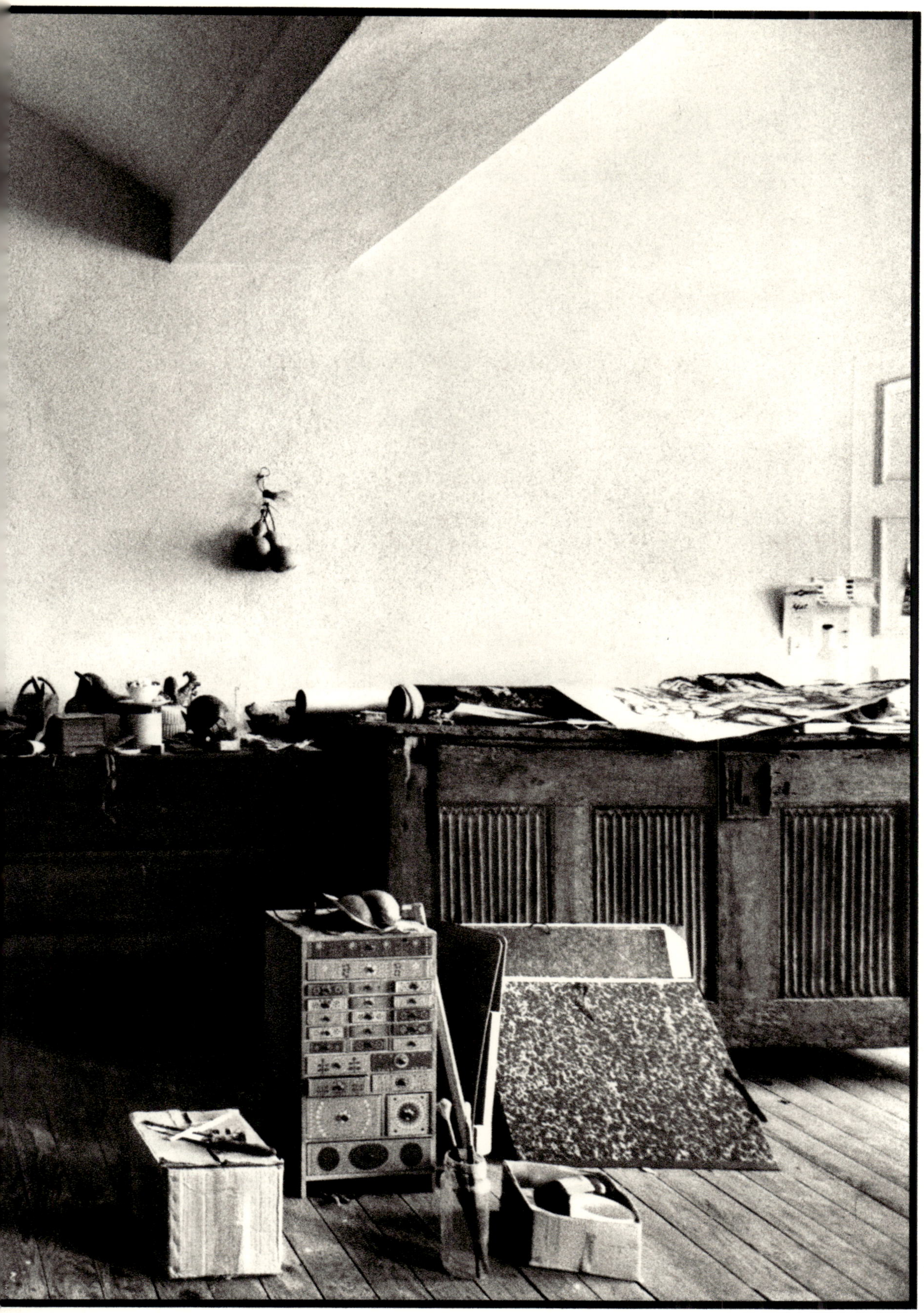

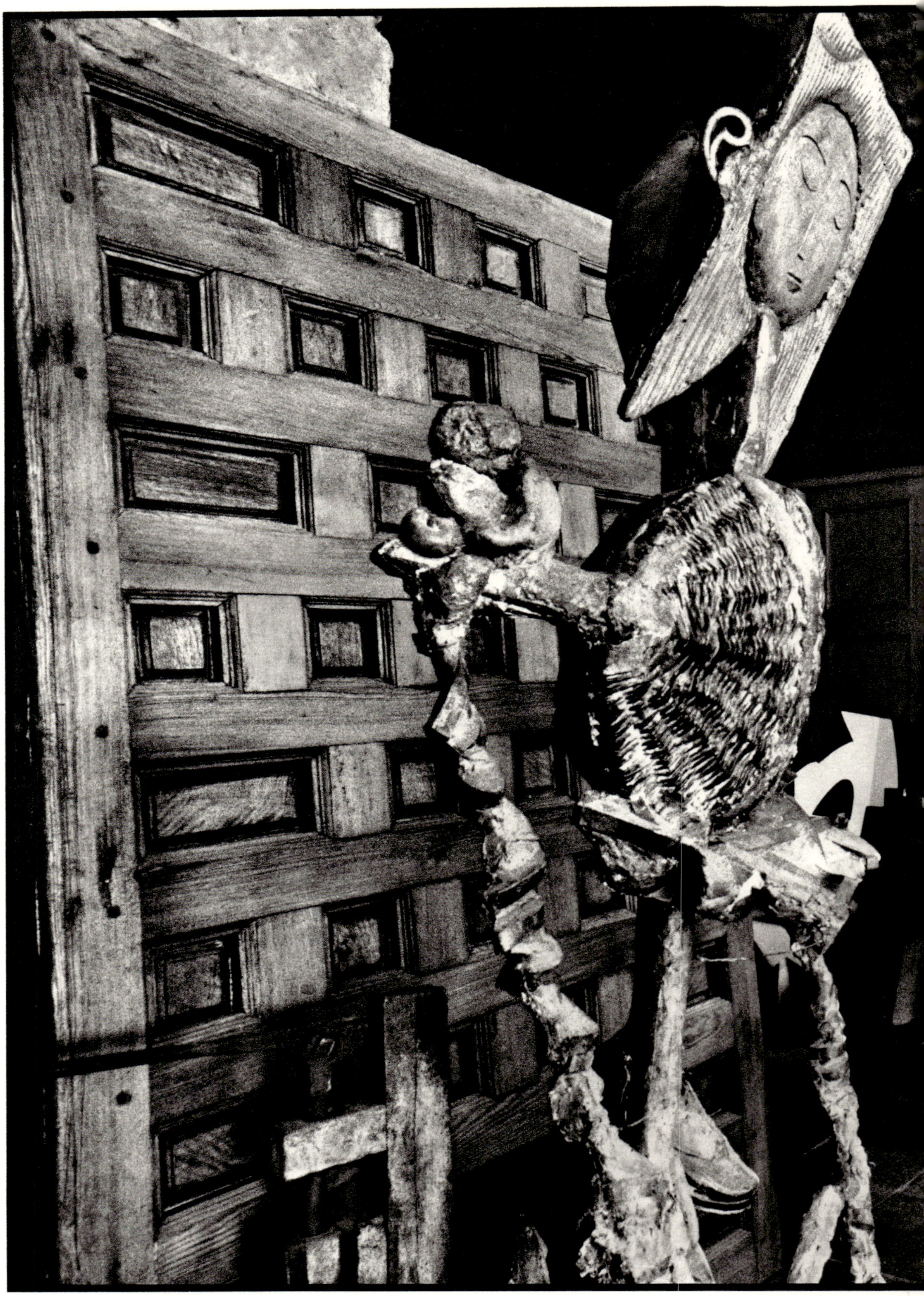

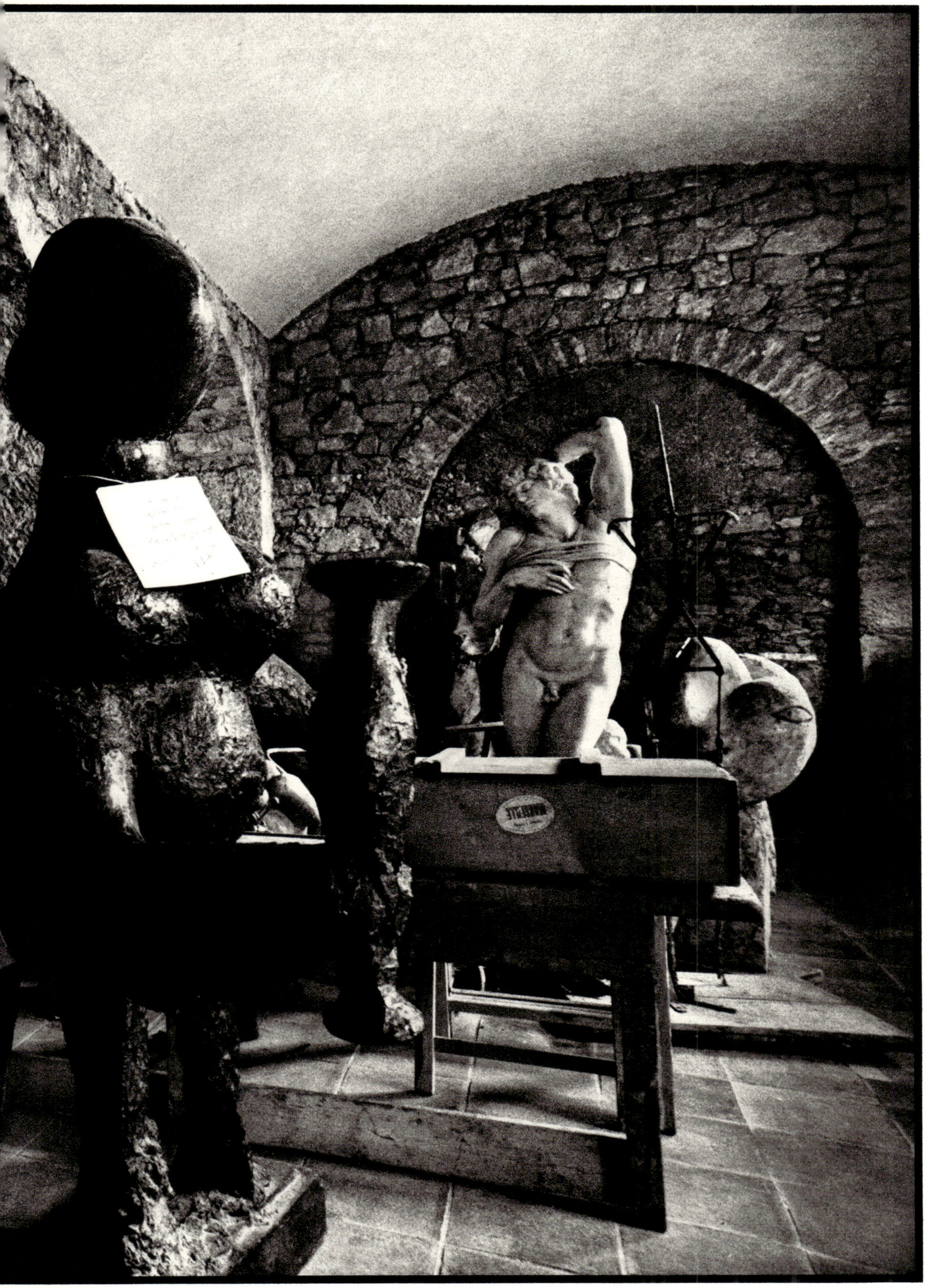

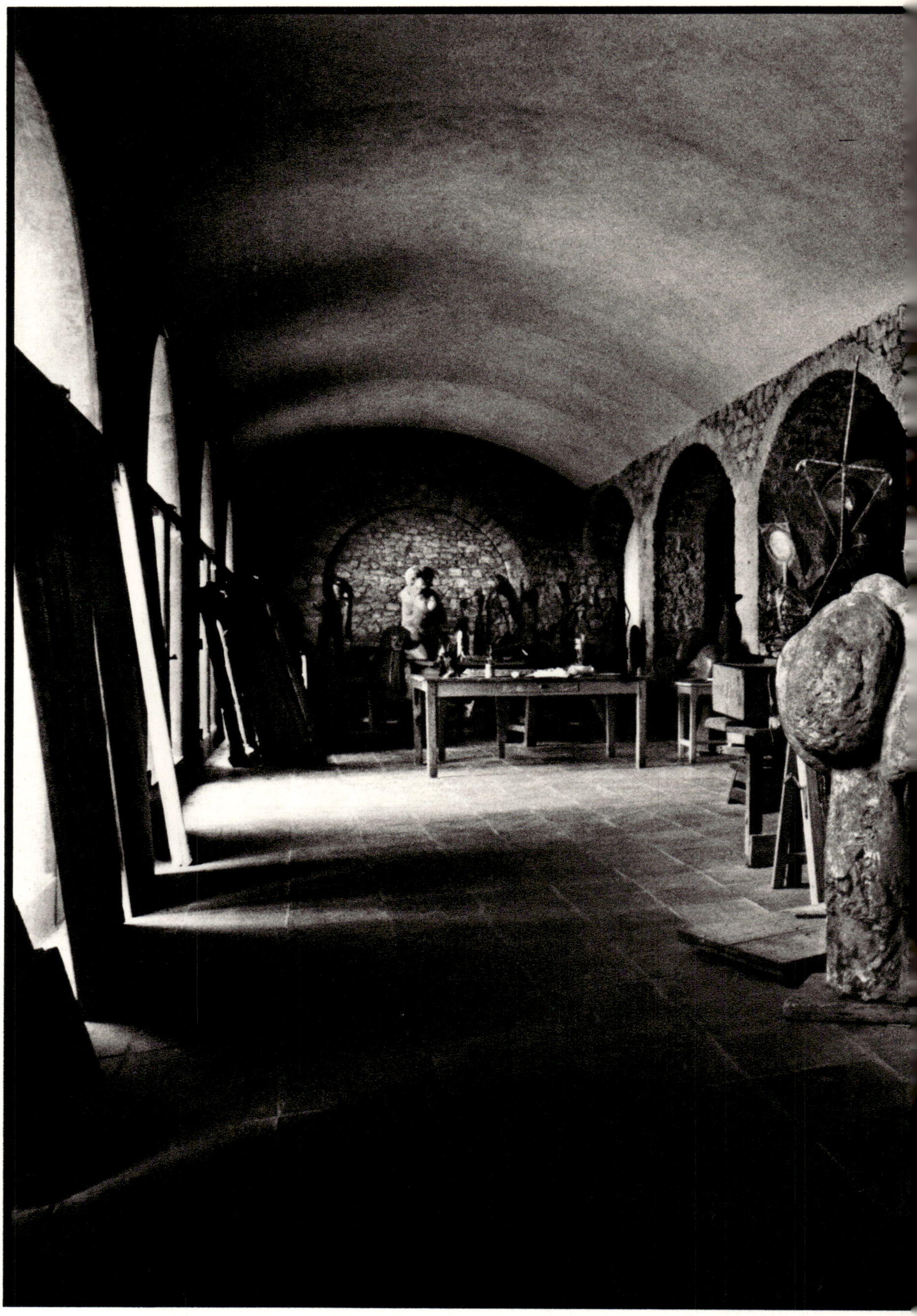

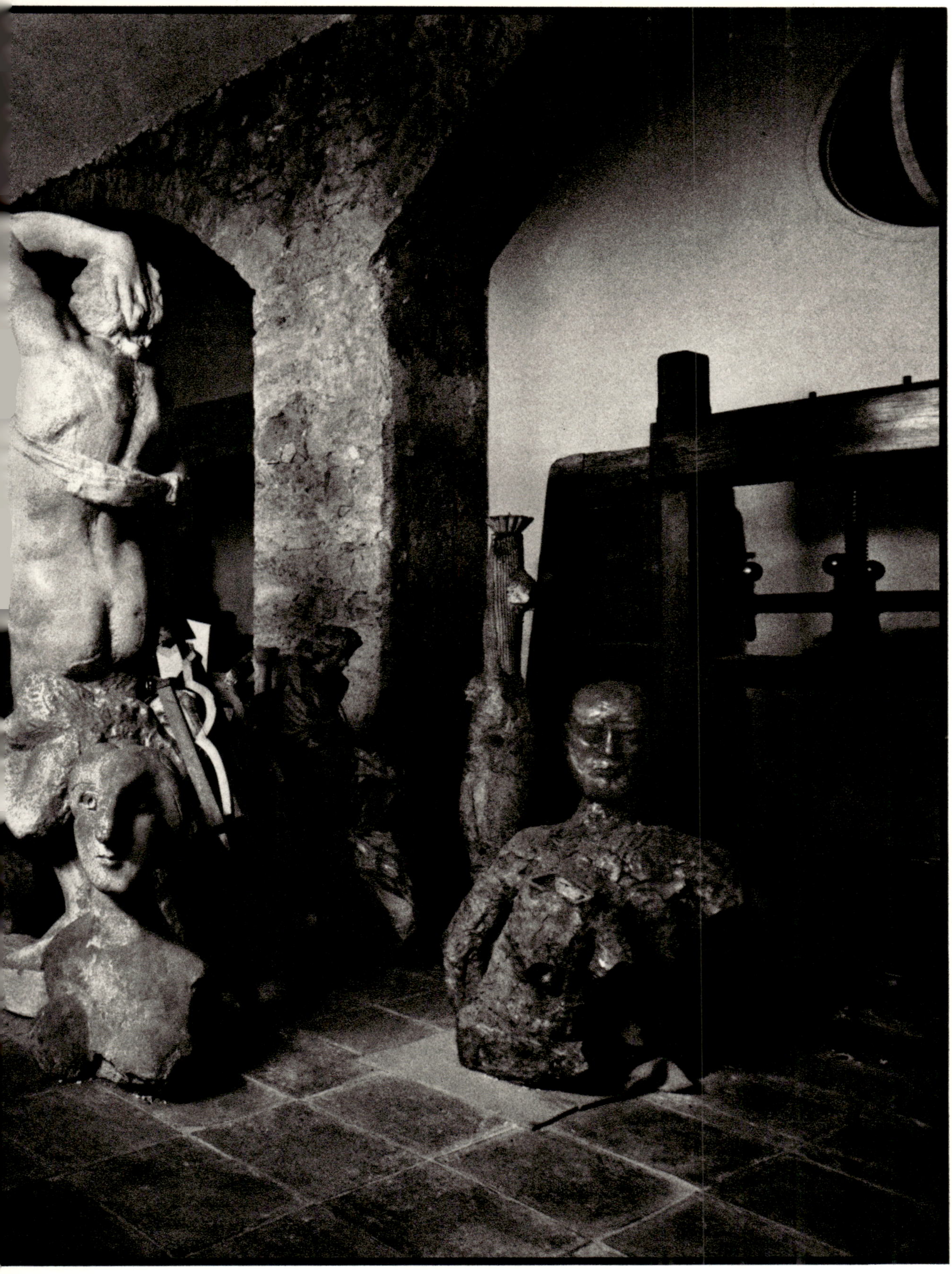

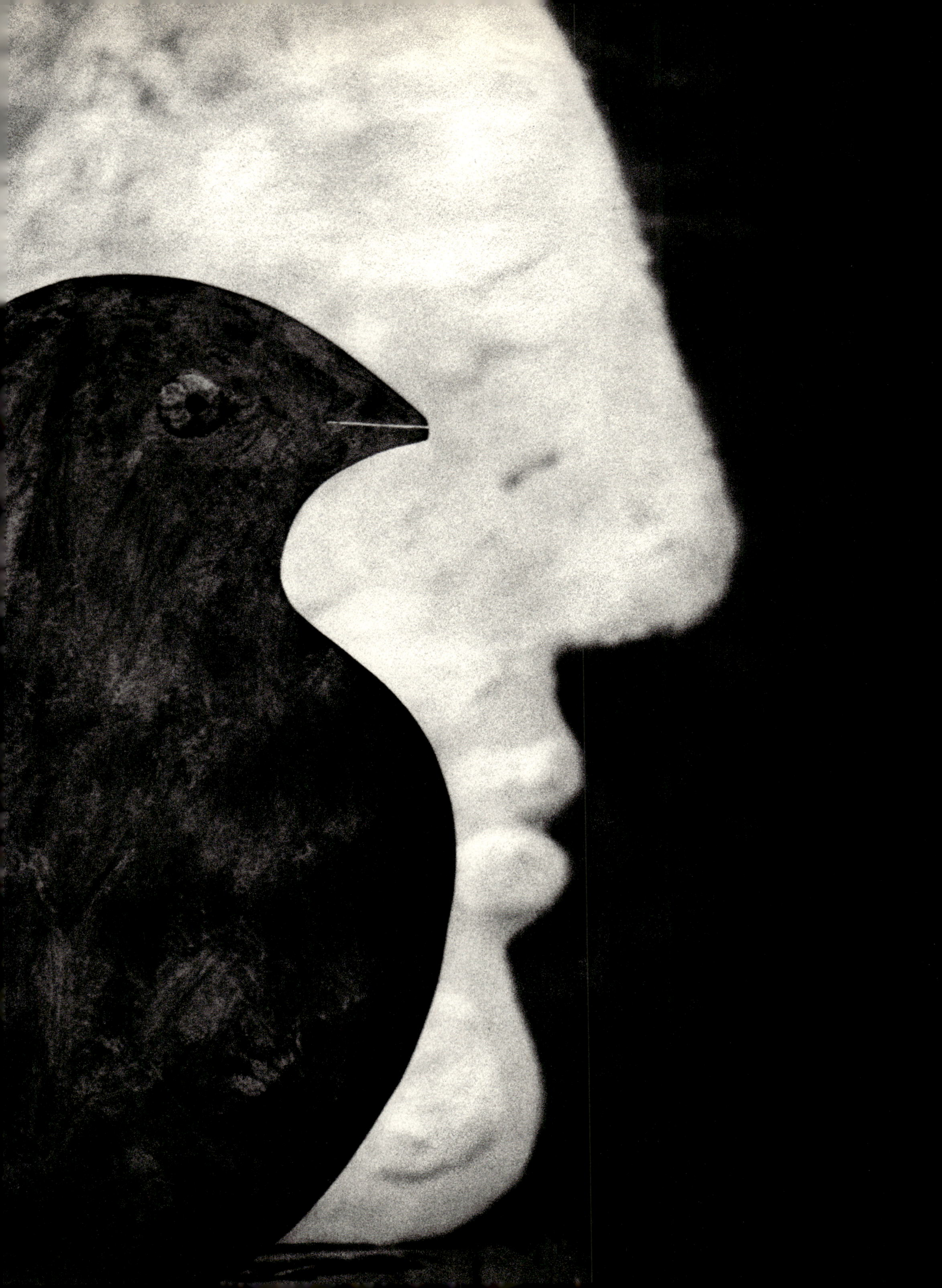

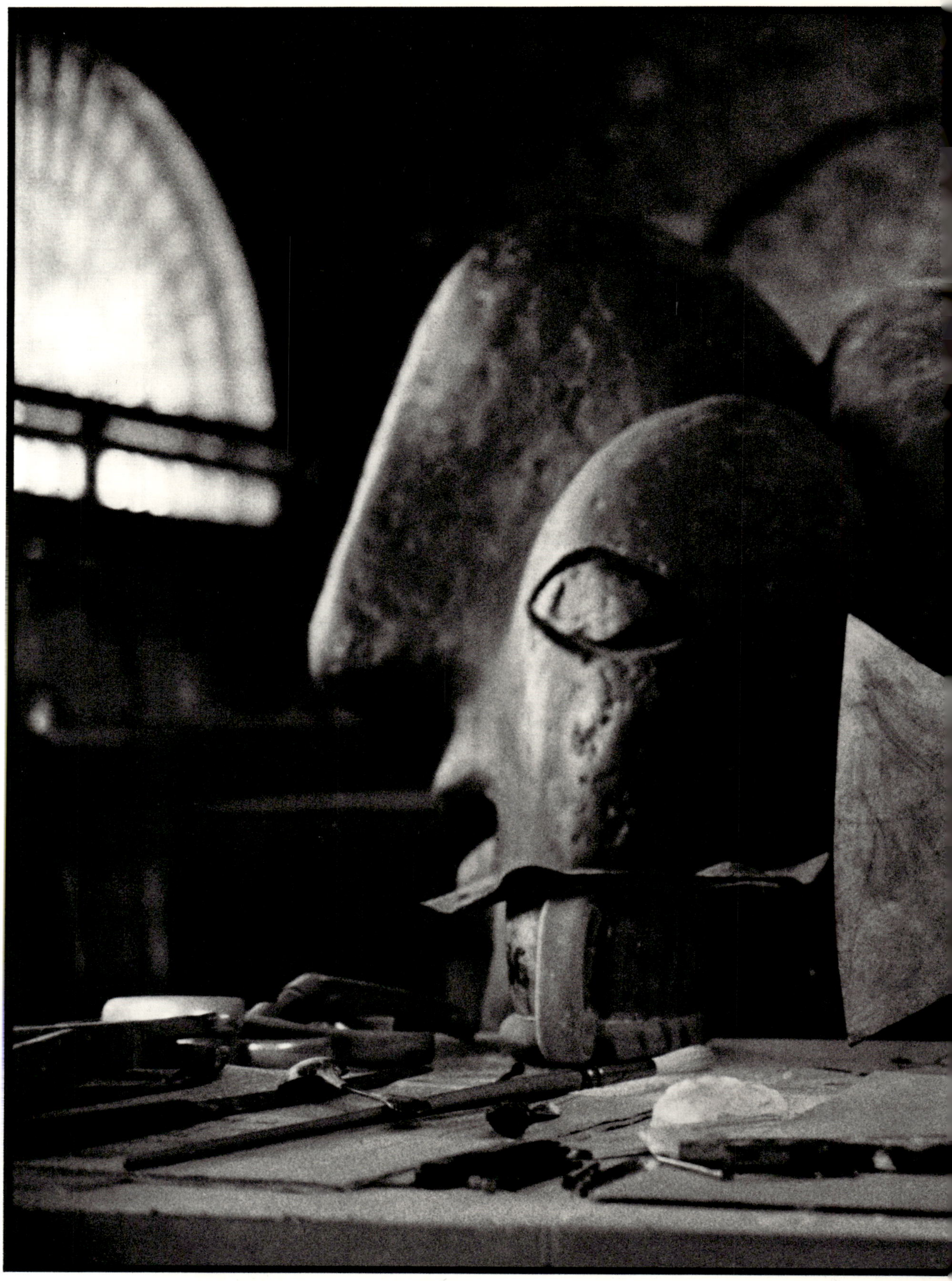

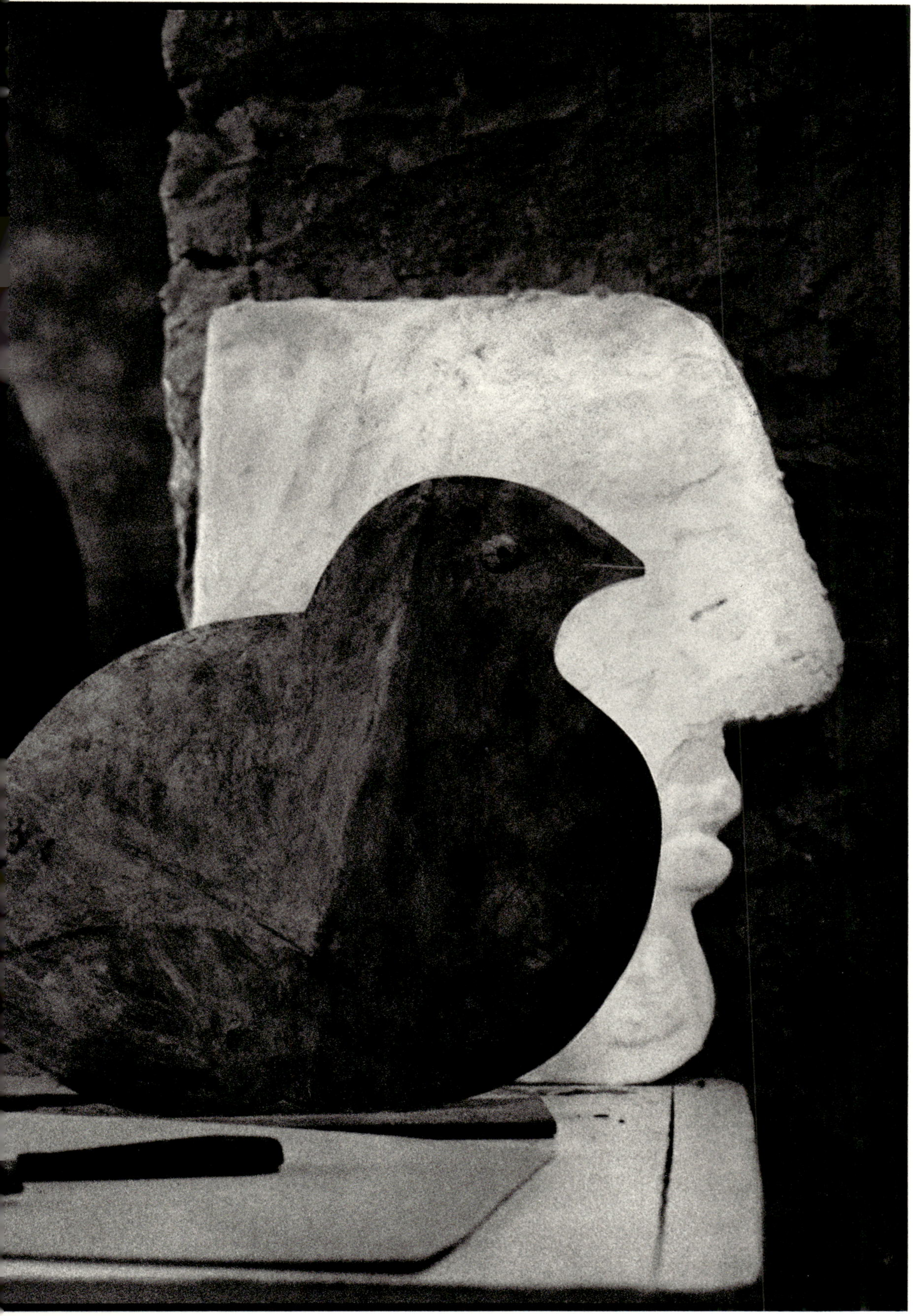

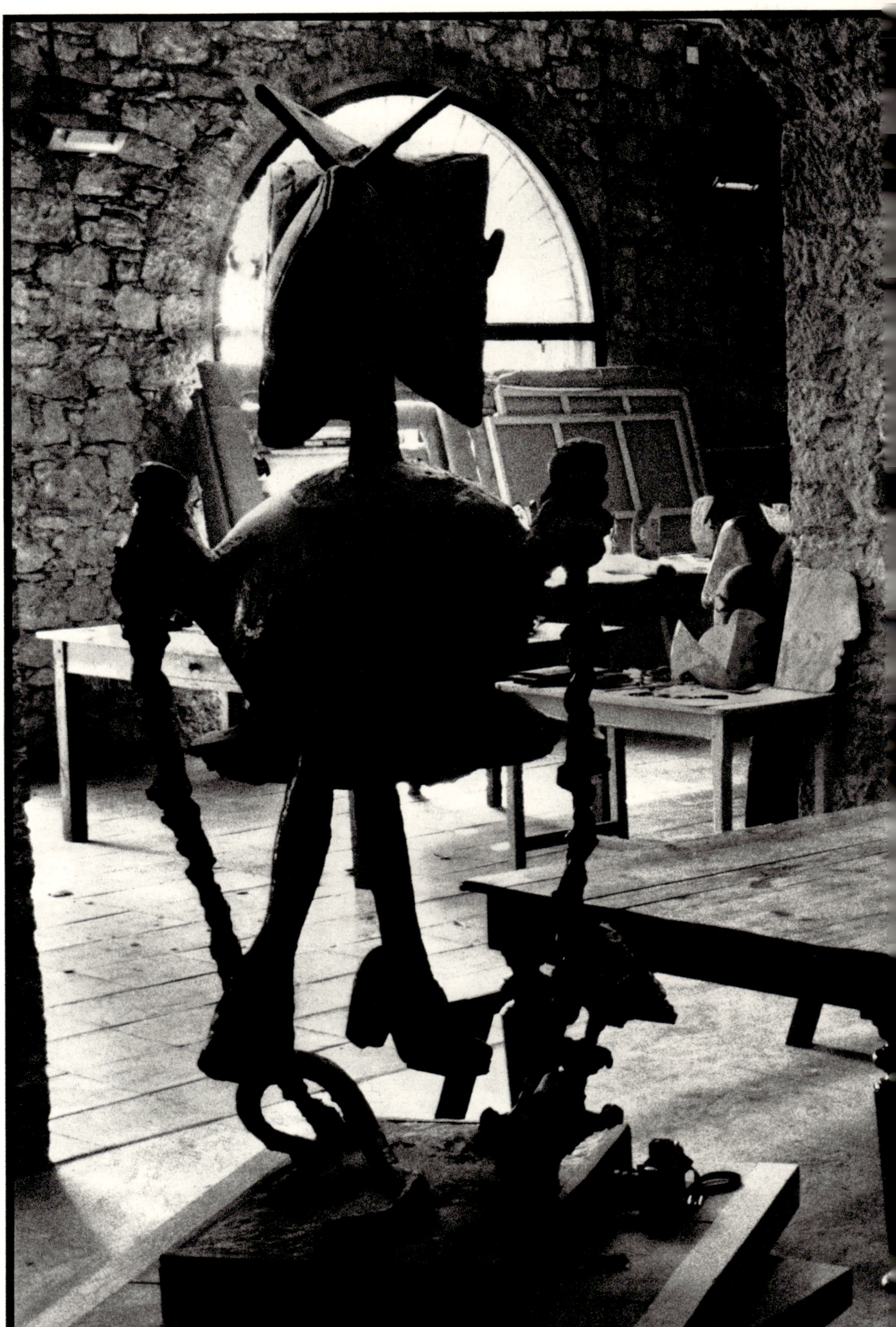

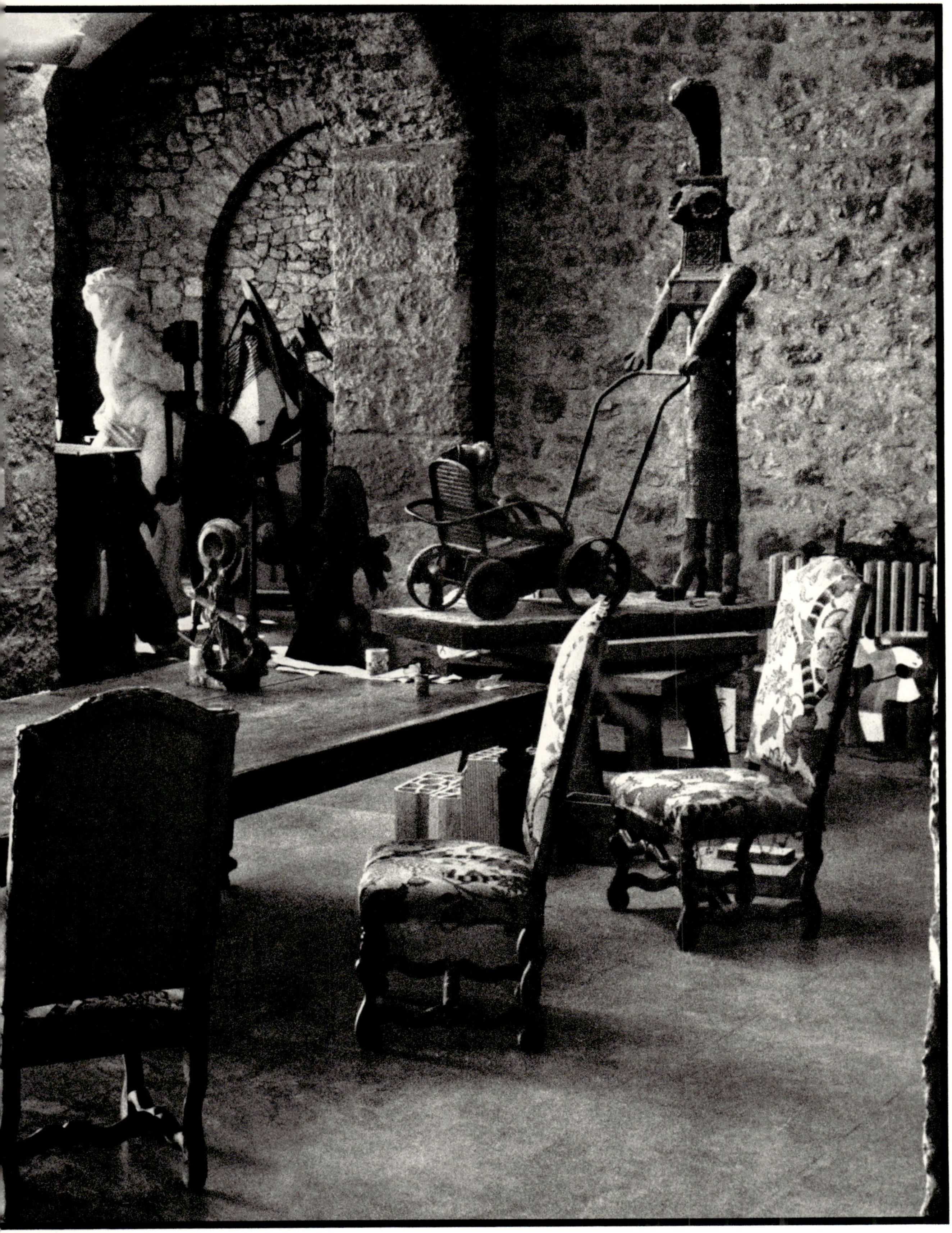

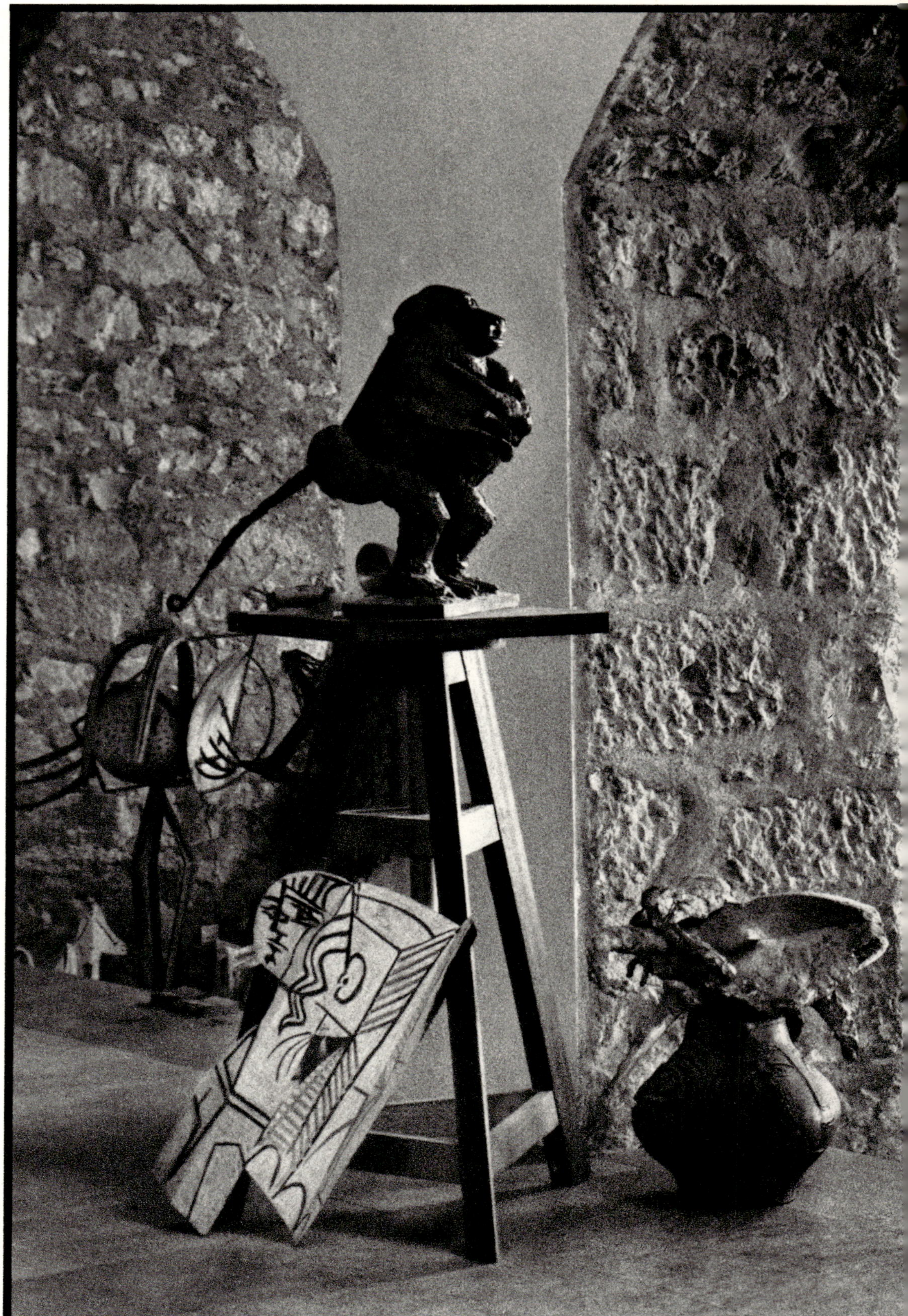

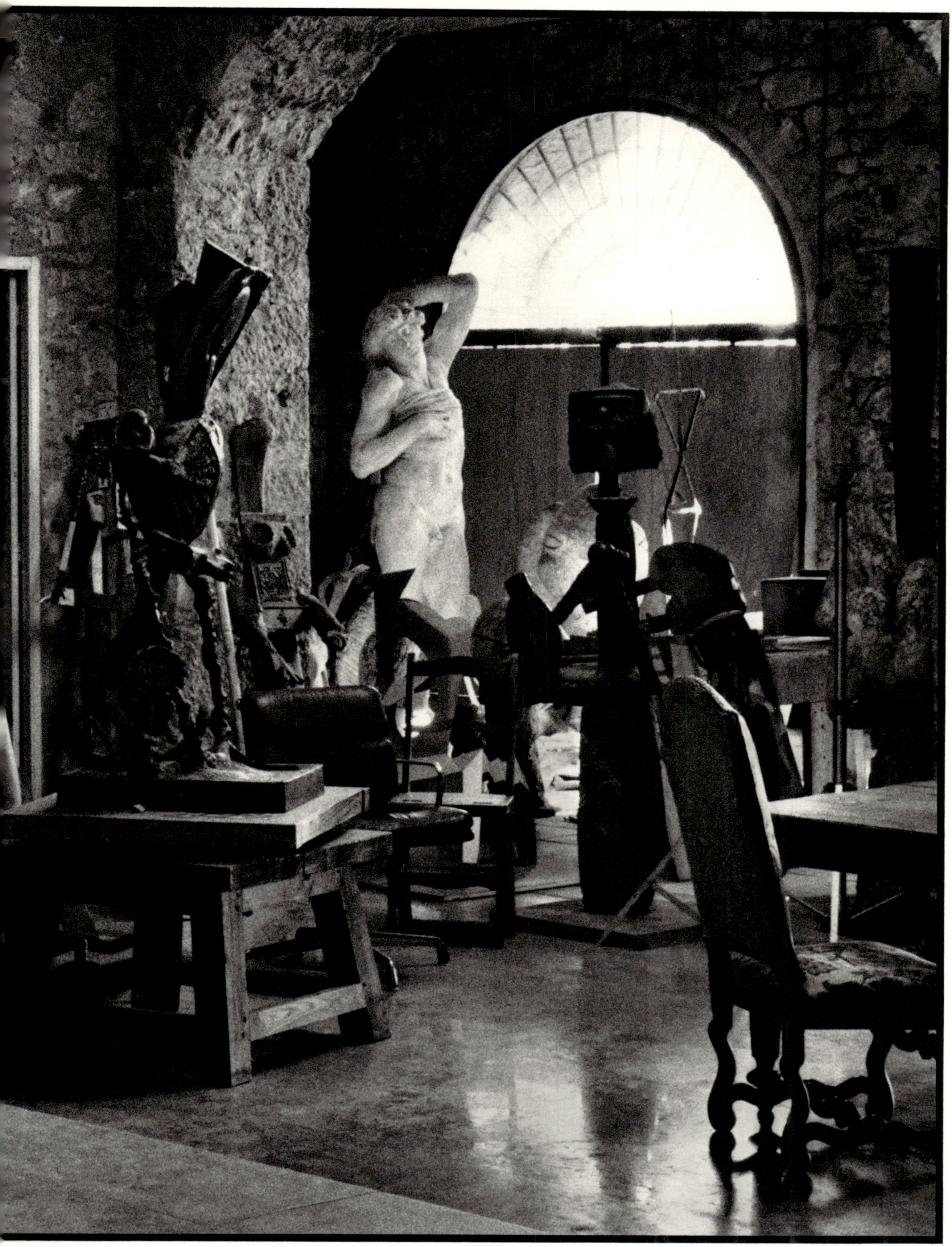

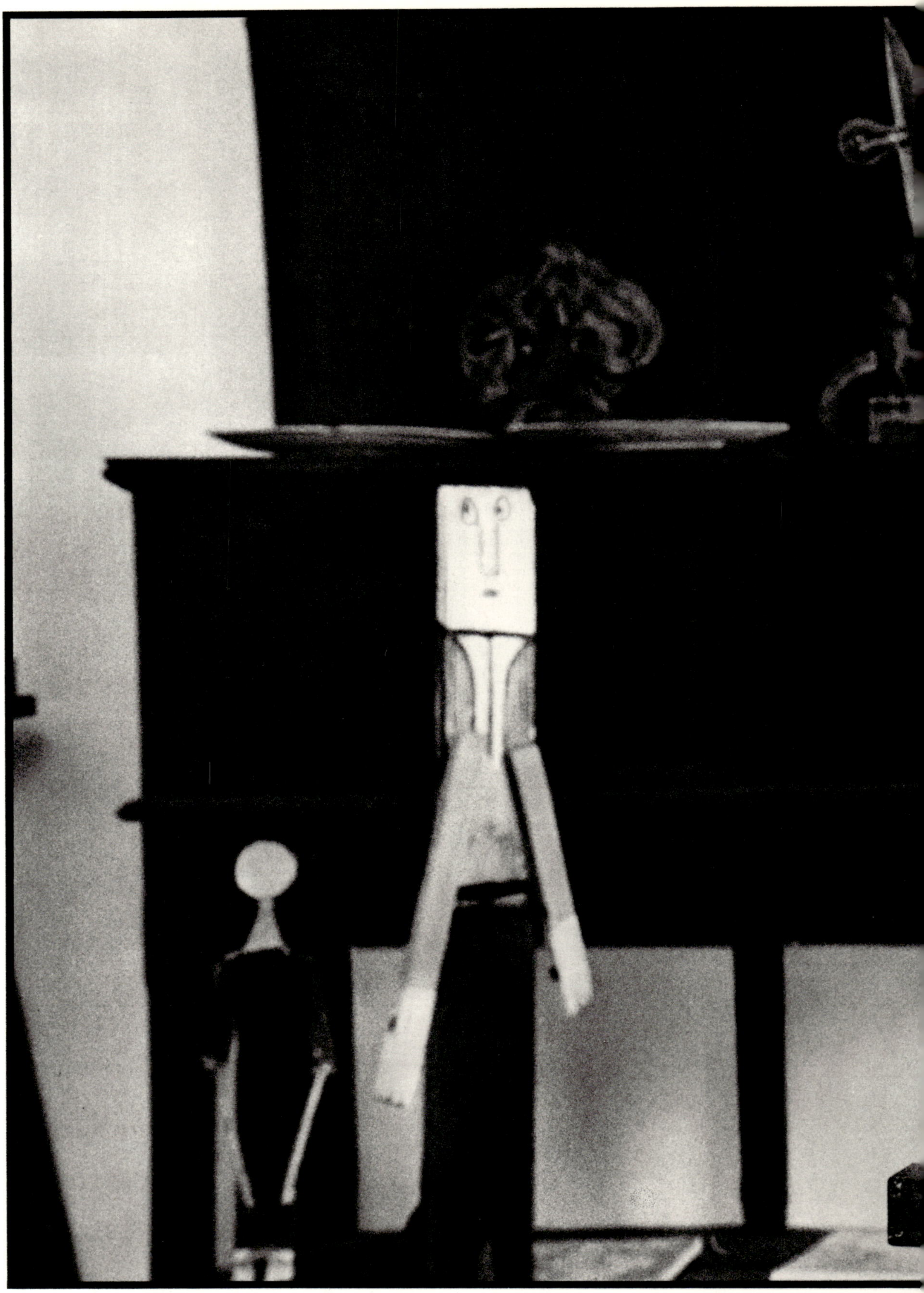

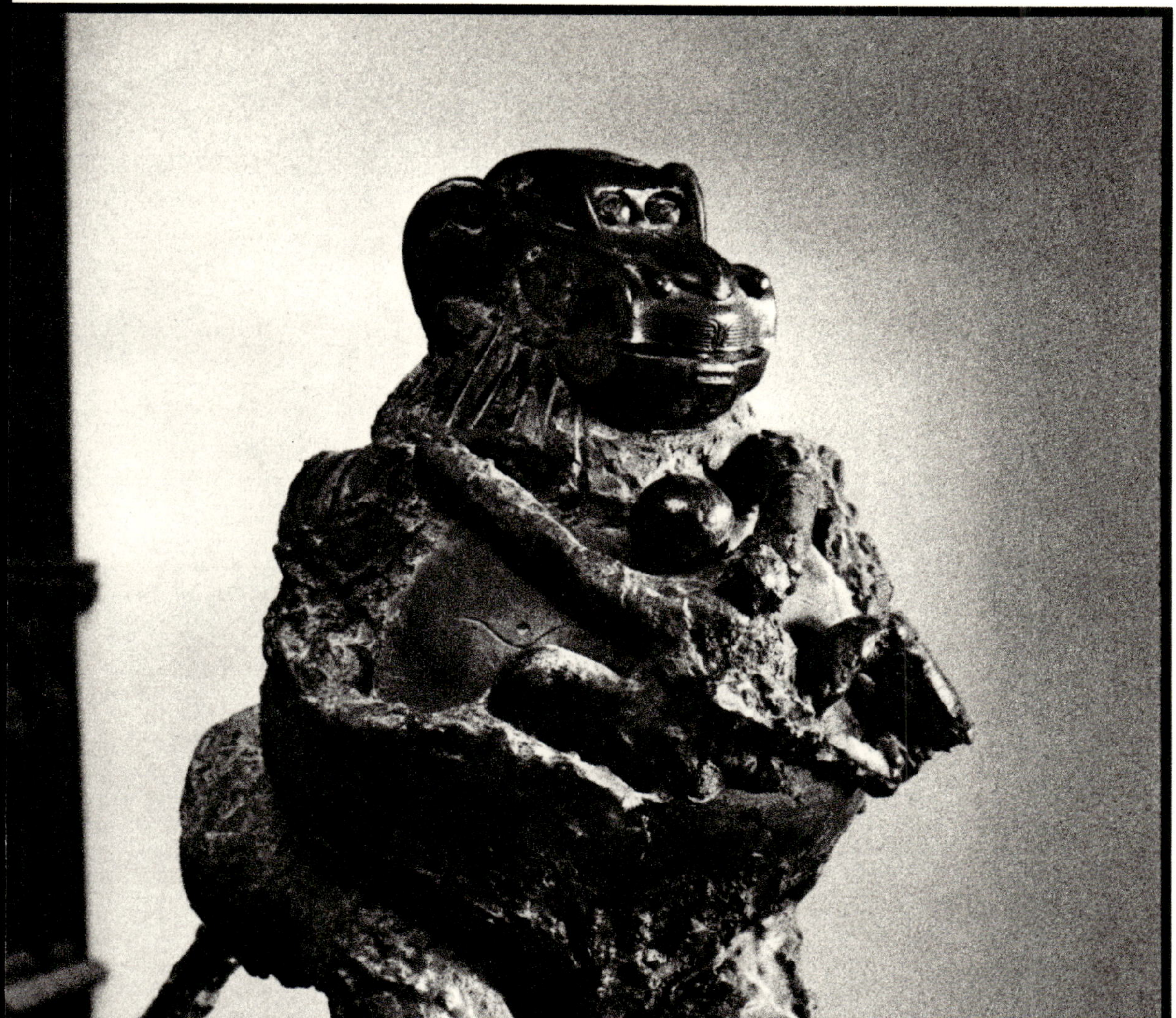

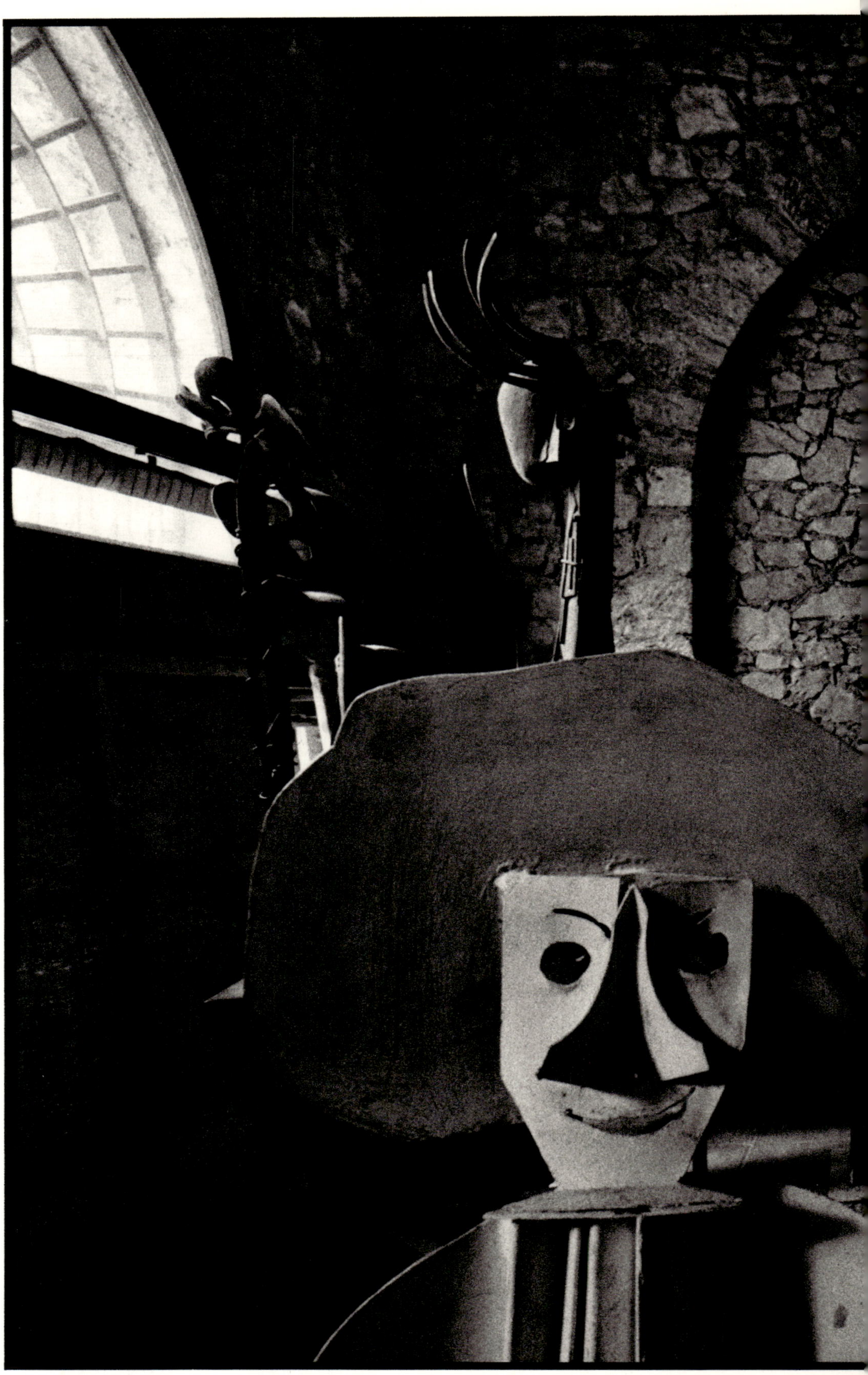

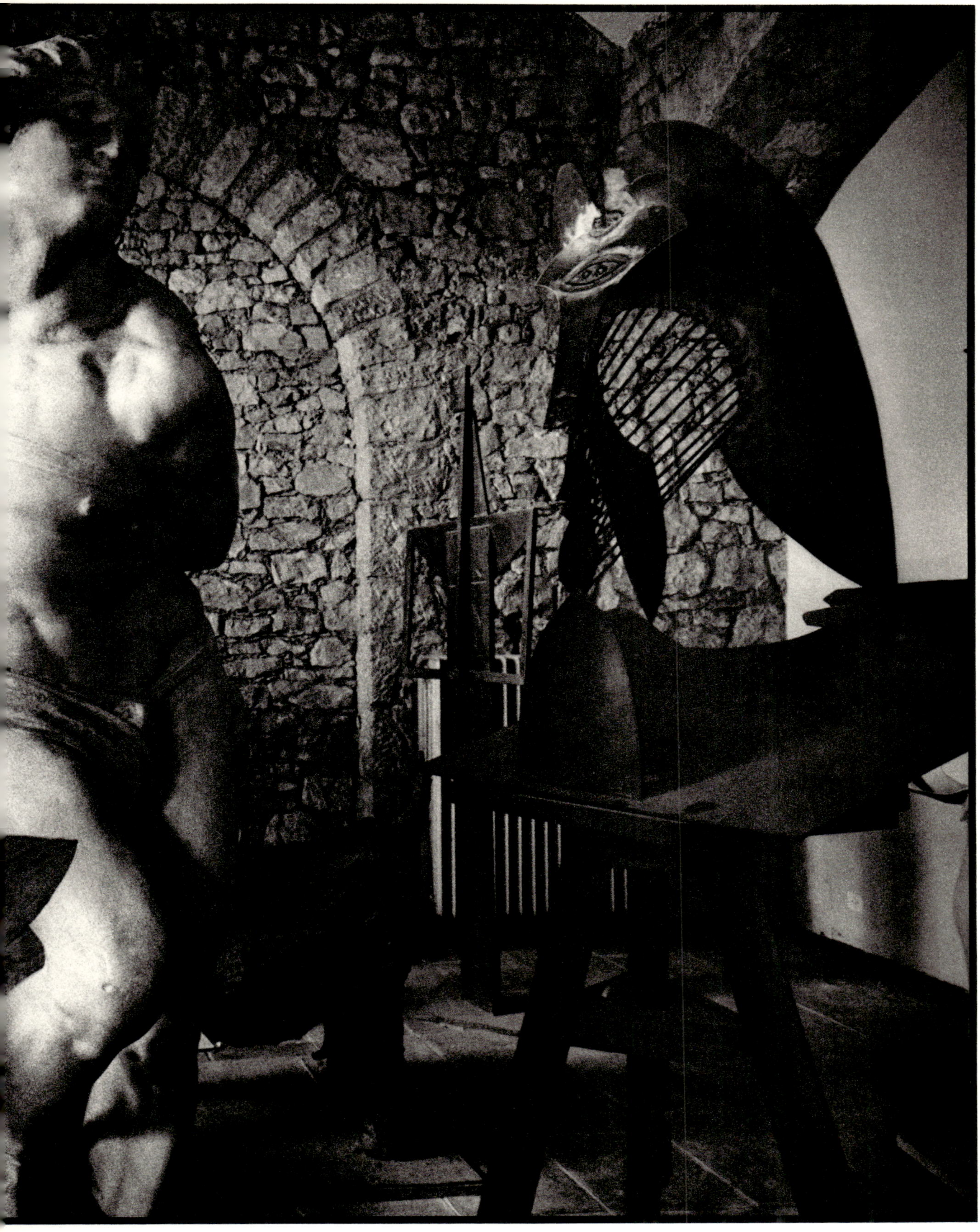

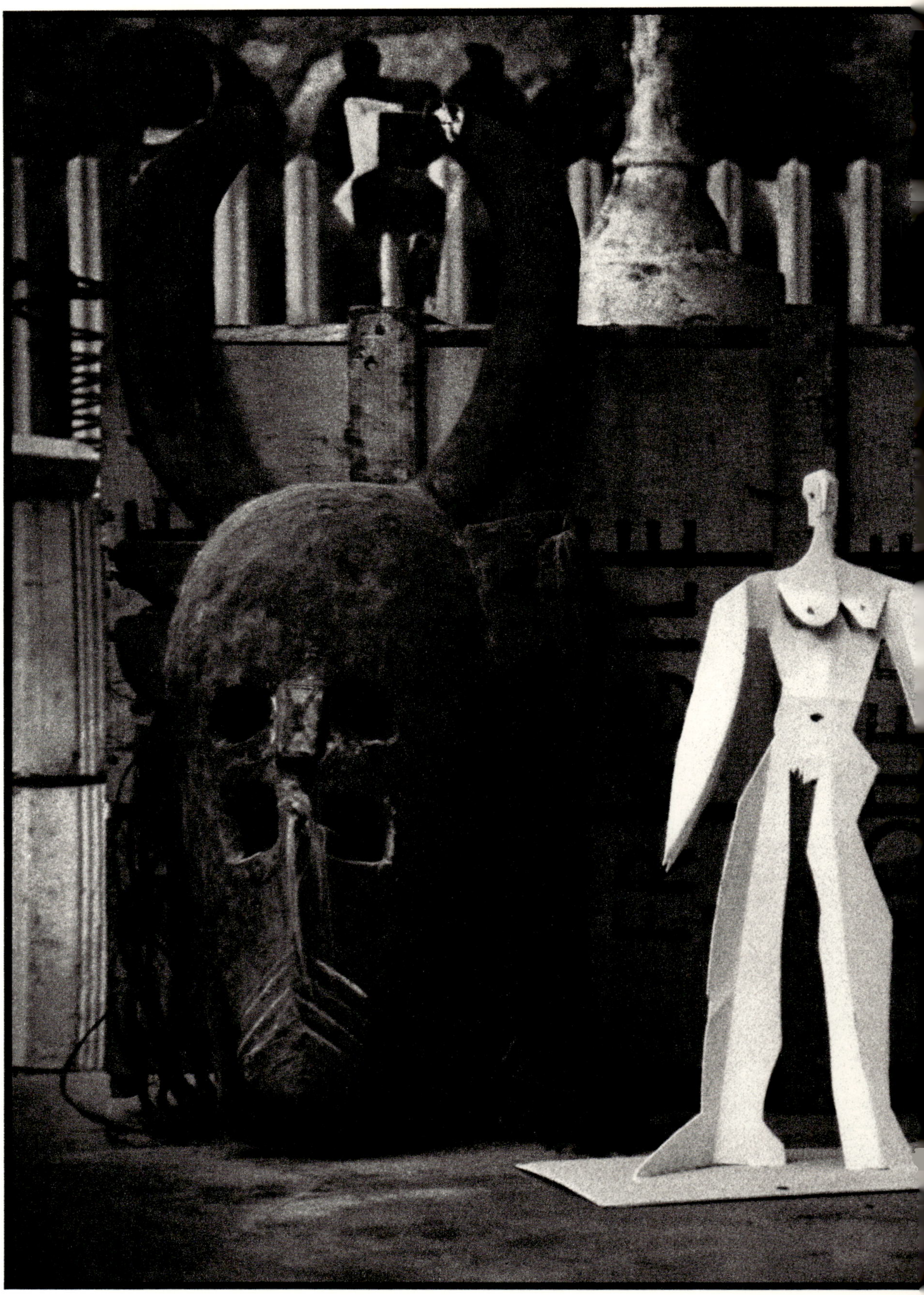

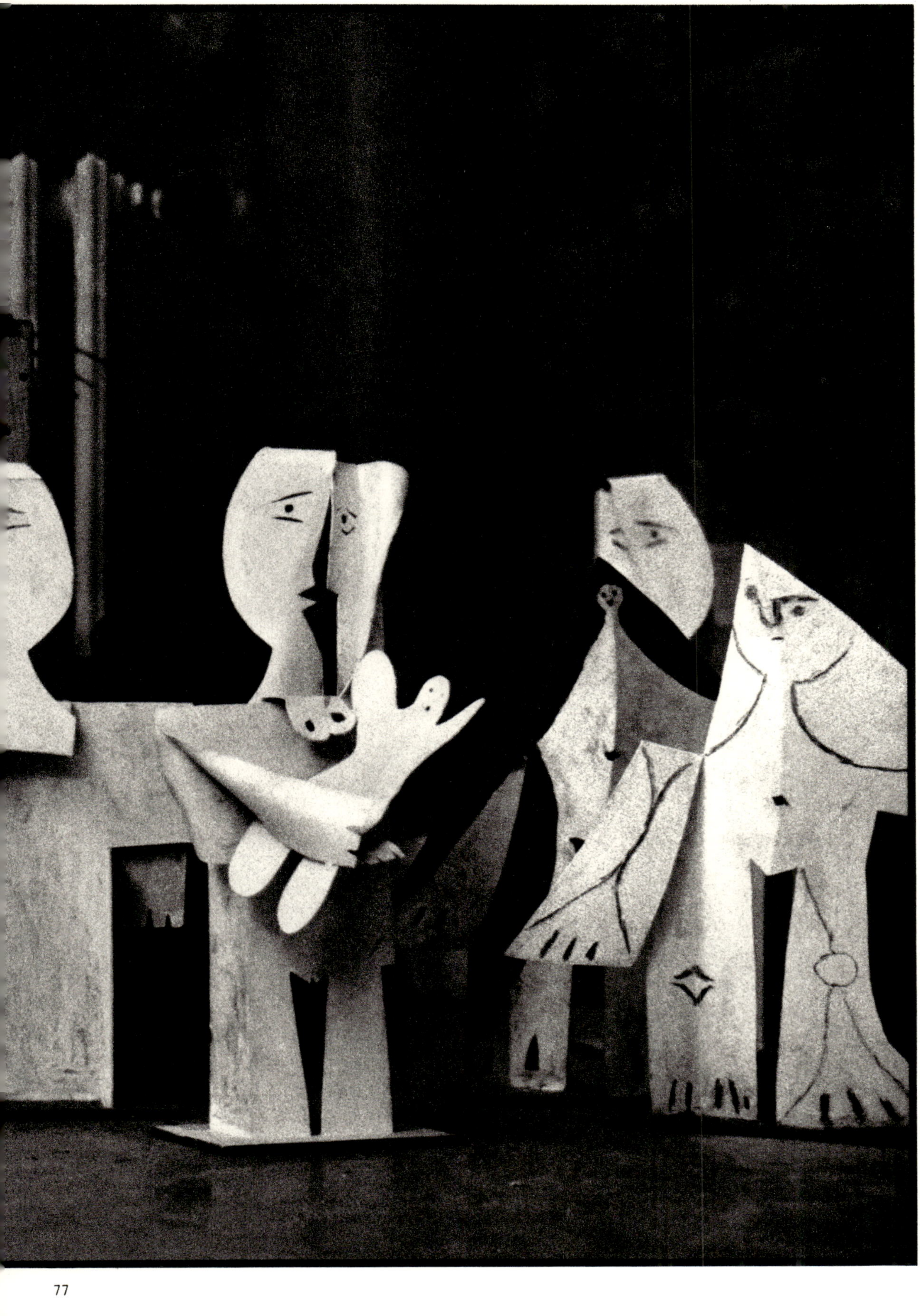

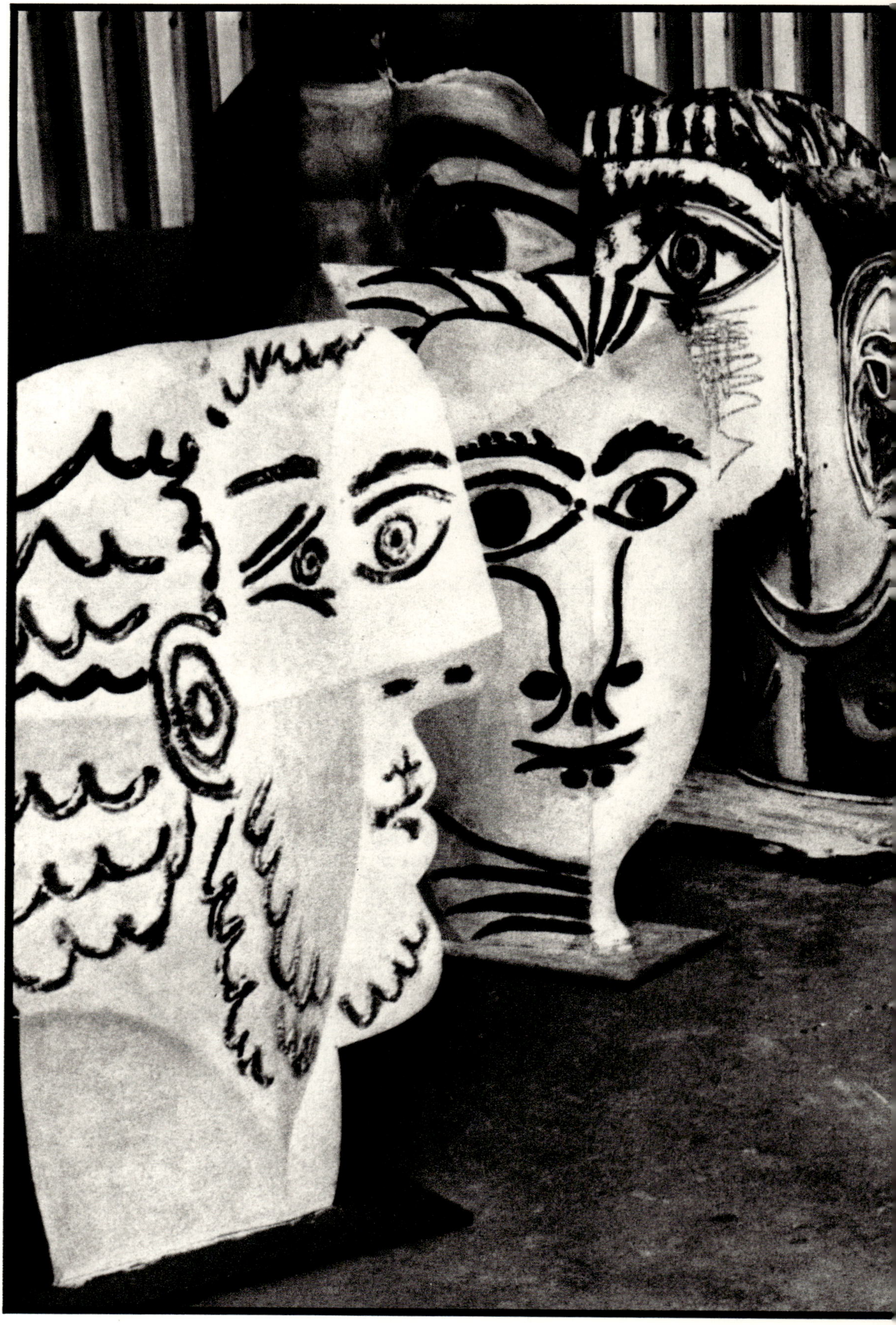

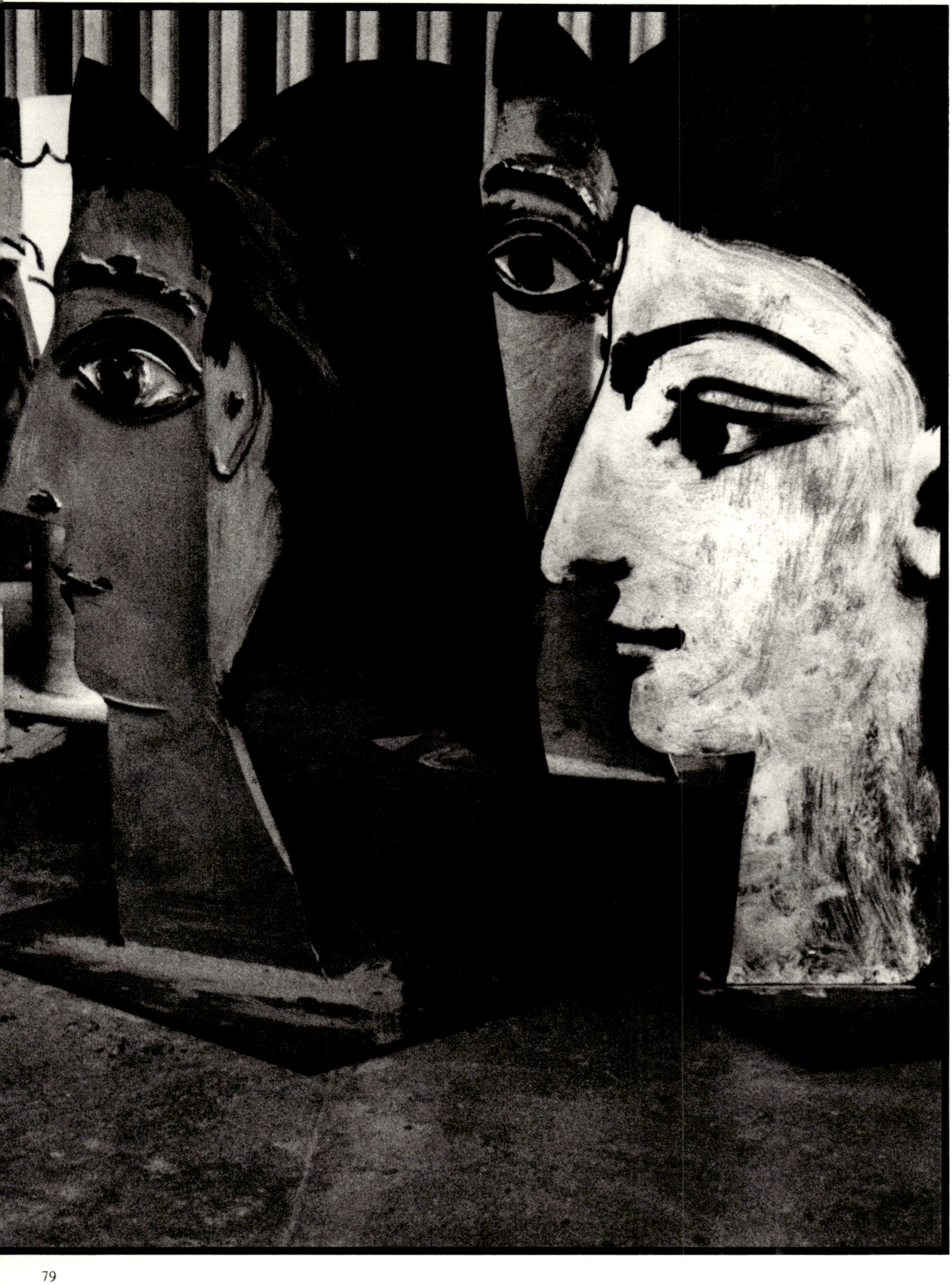

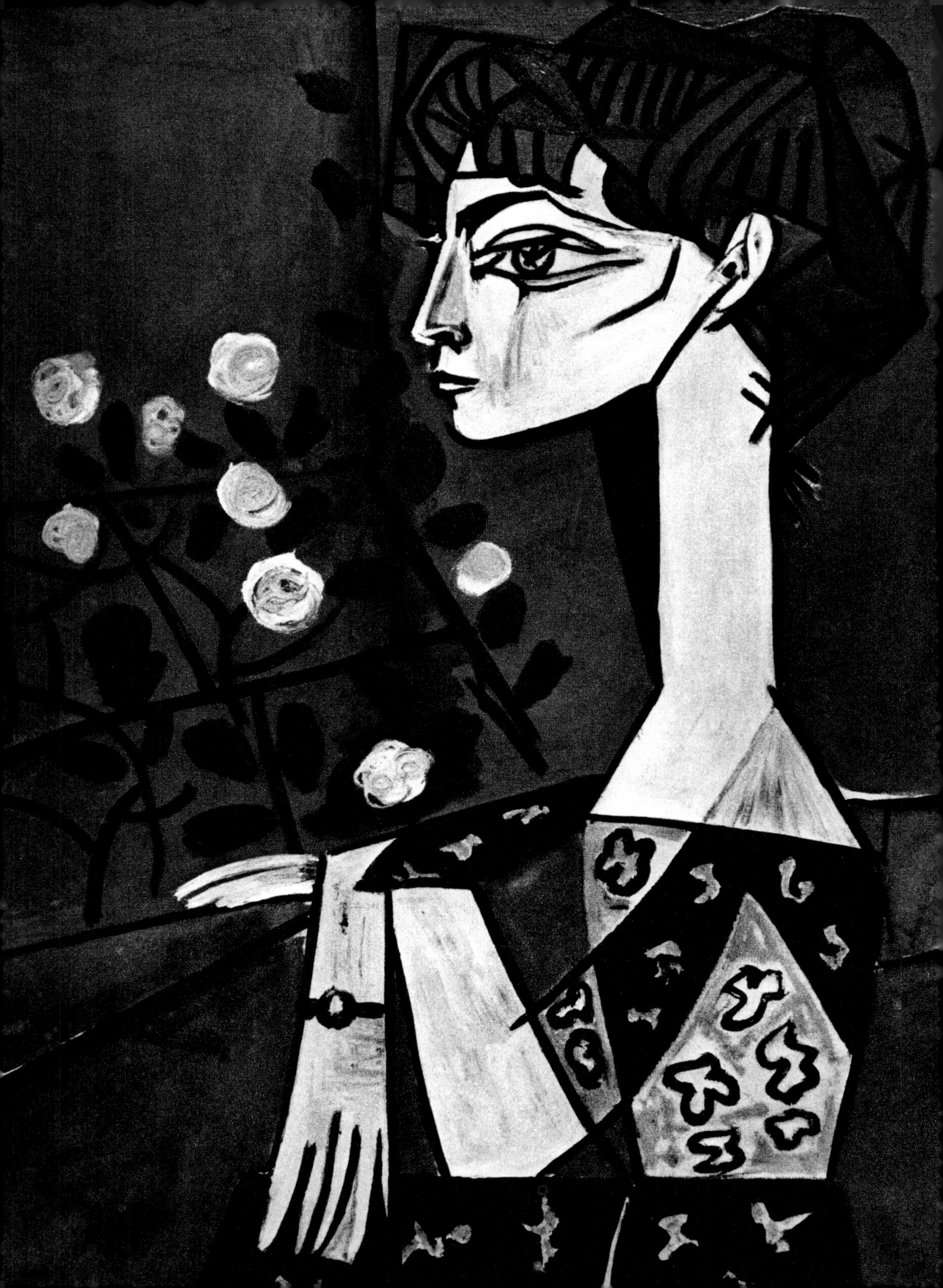

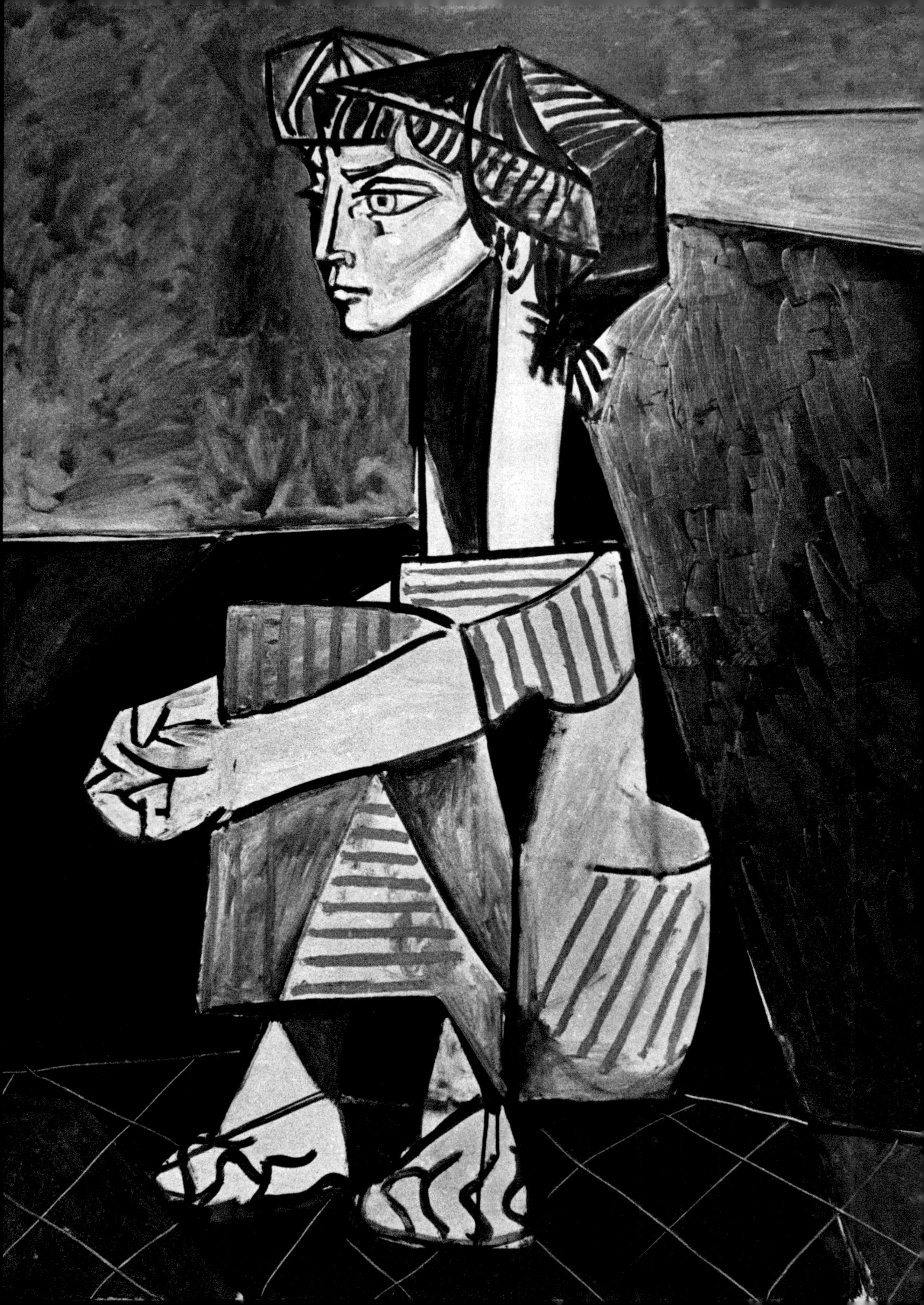

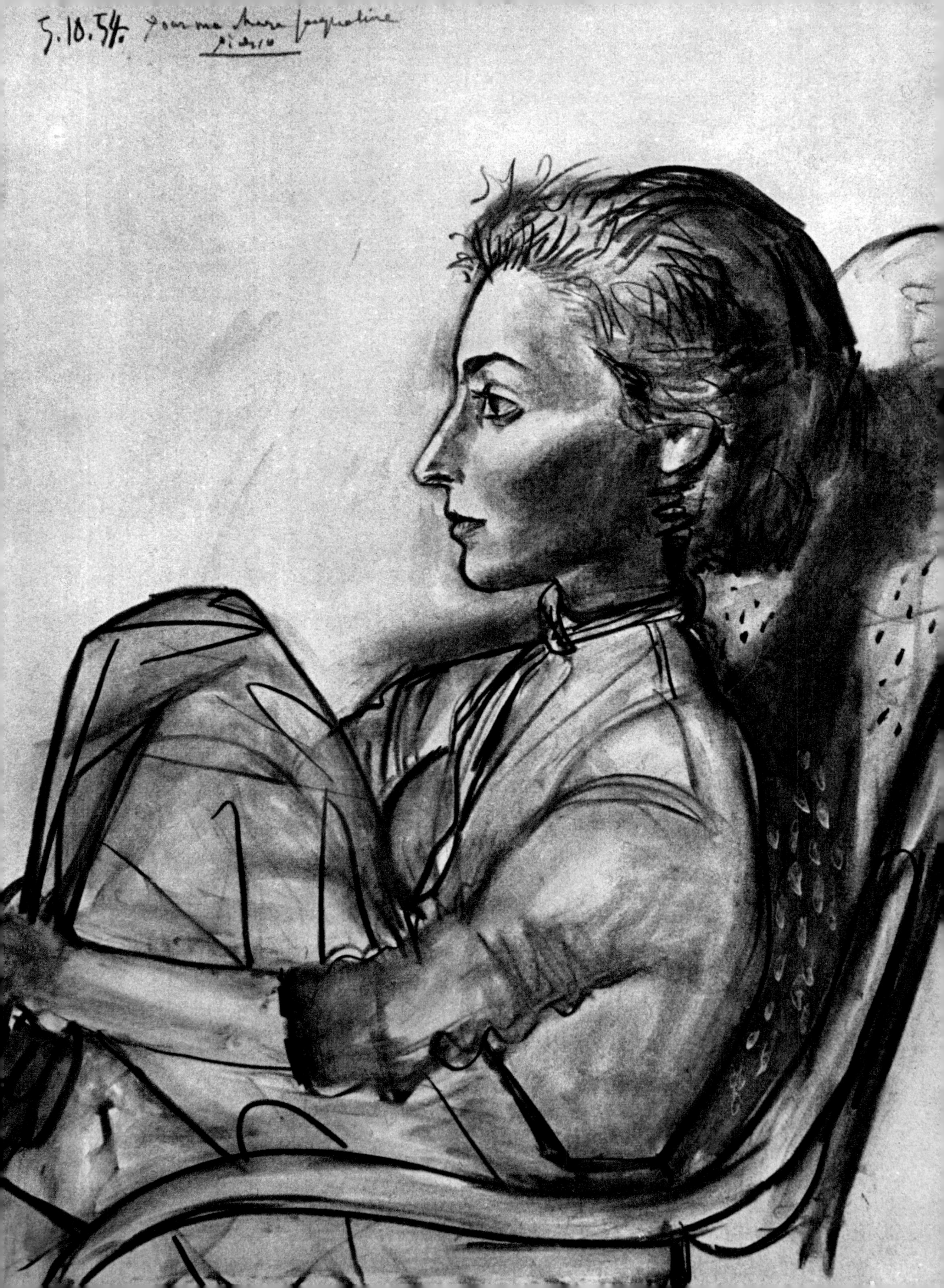
5.10.54.

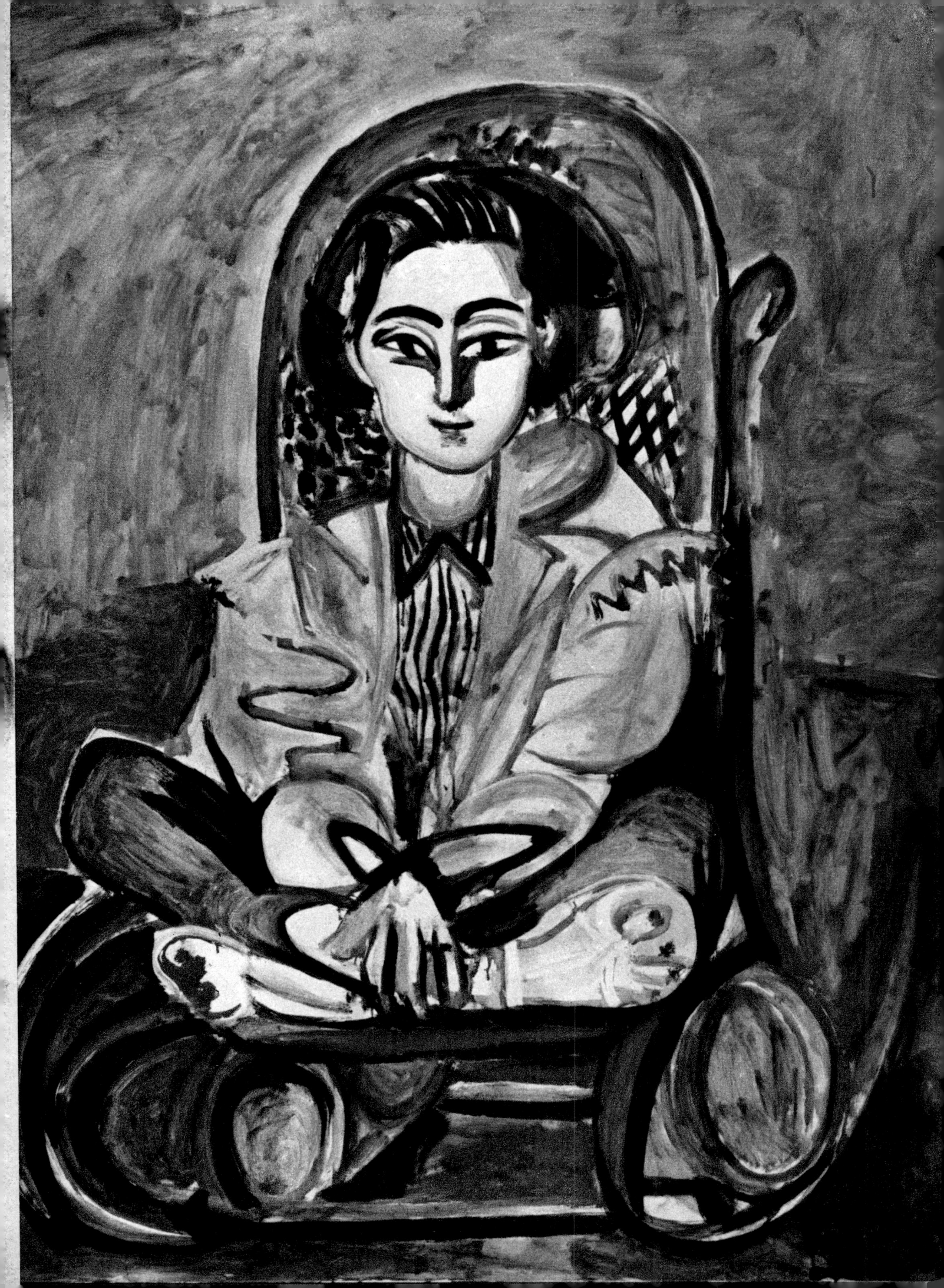

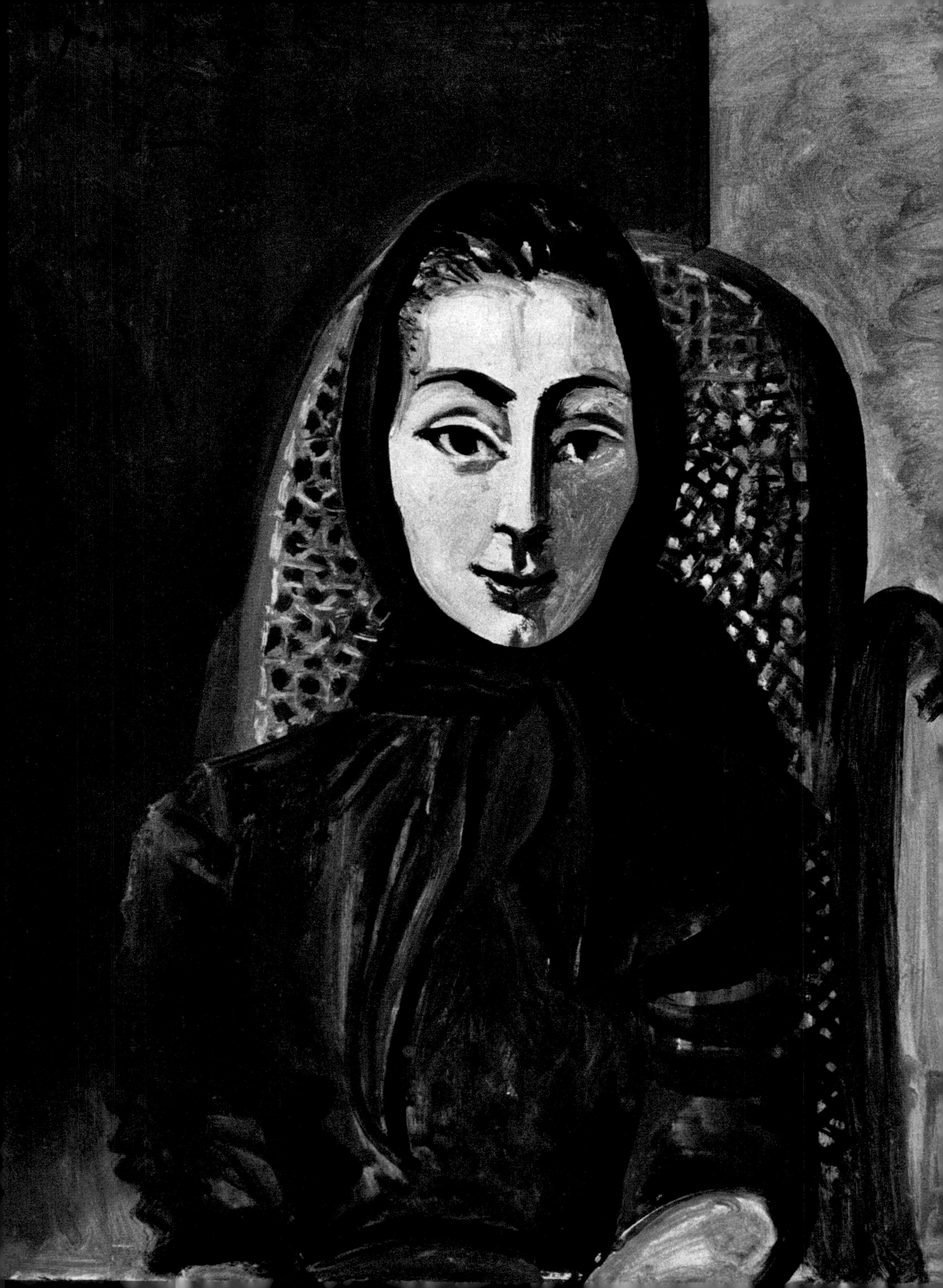

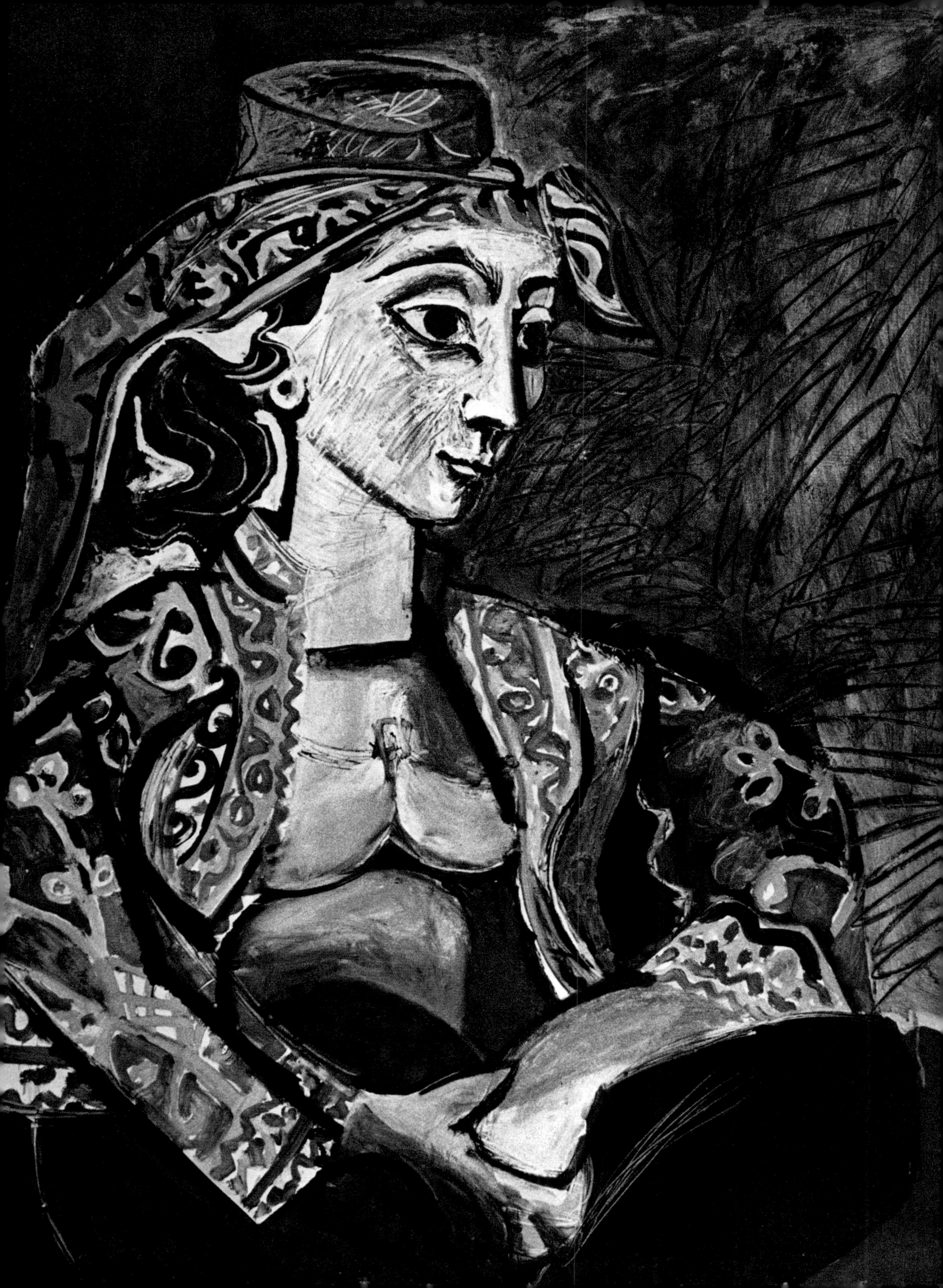

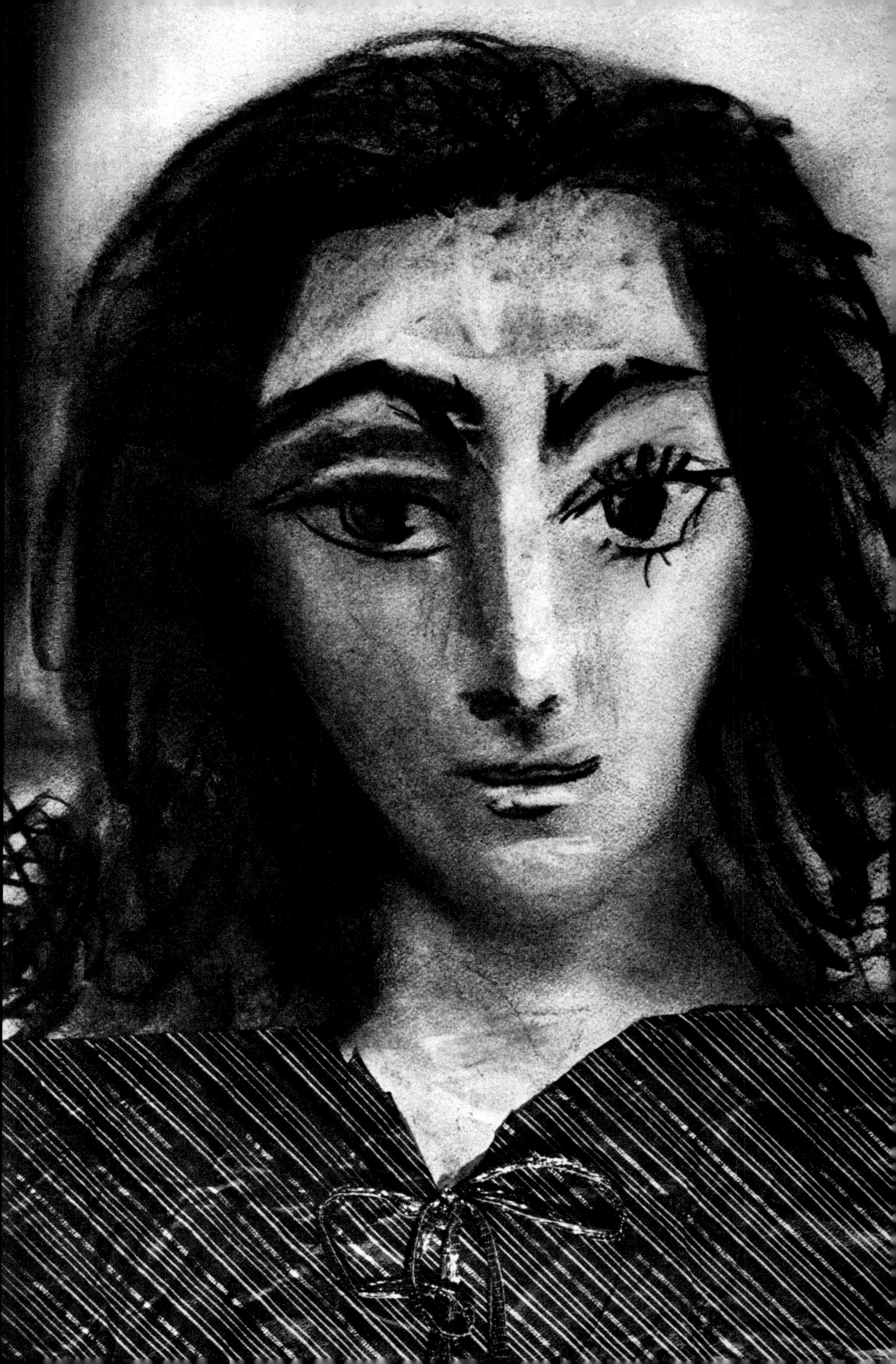

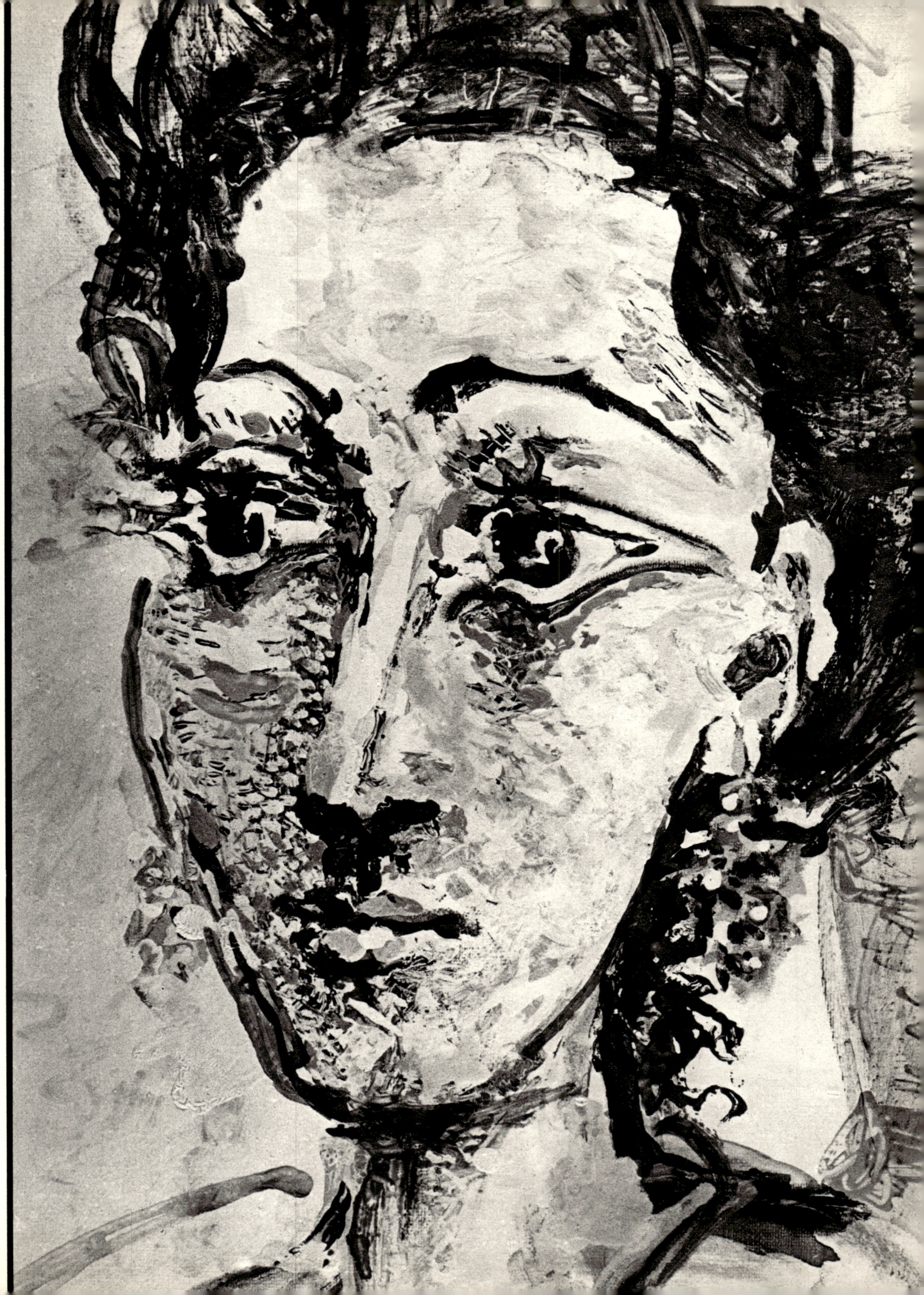

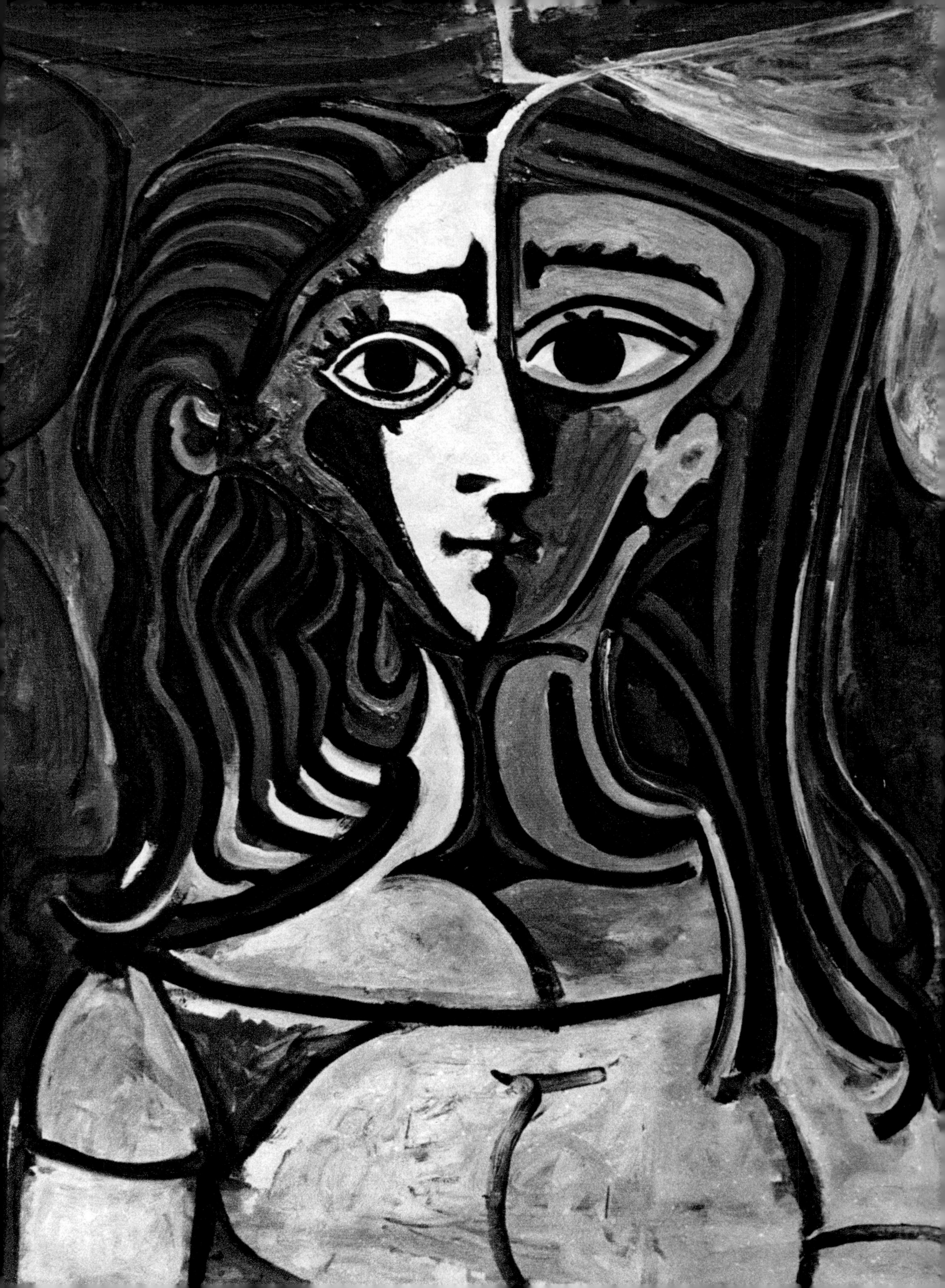

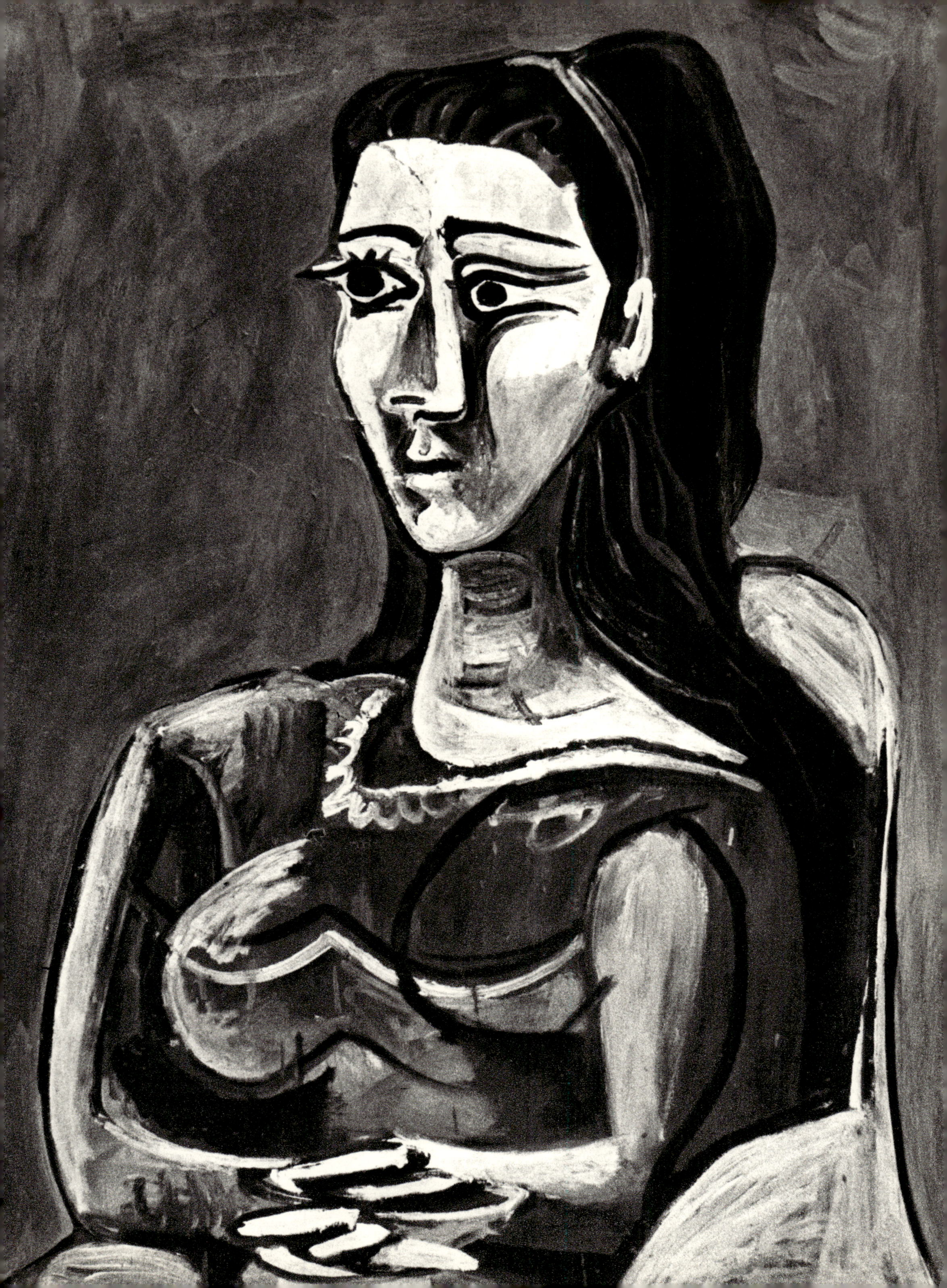

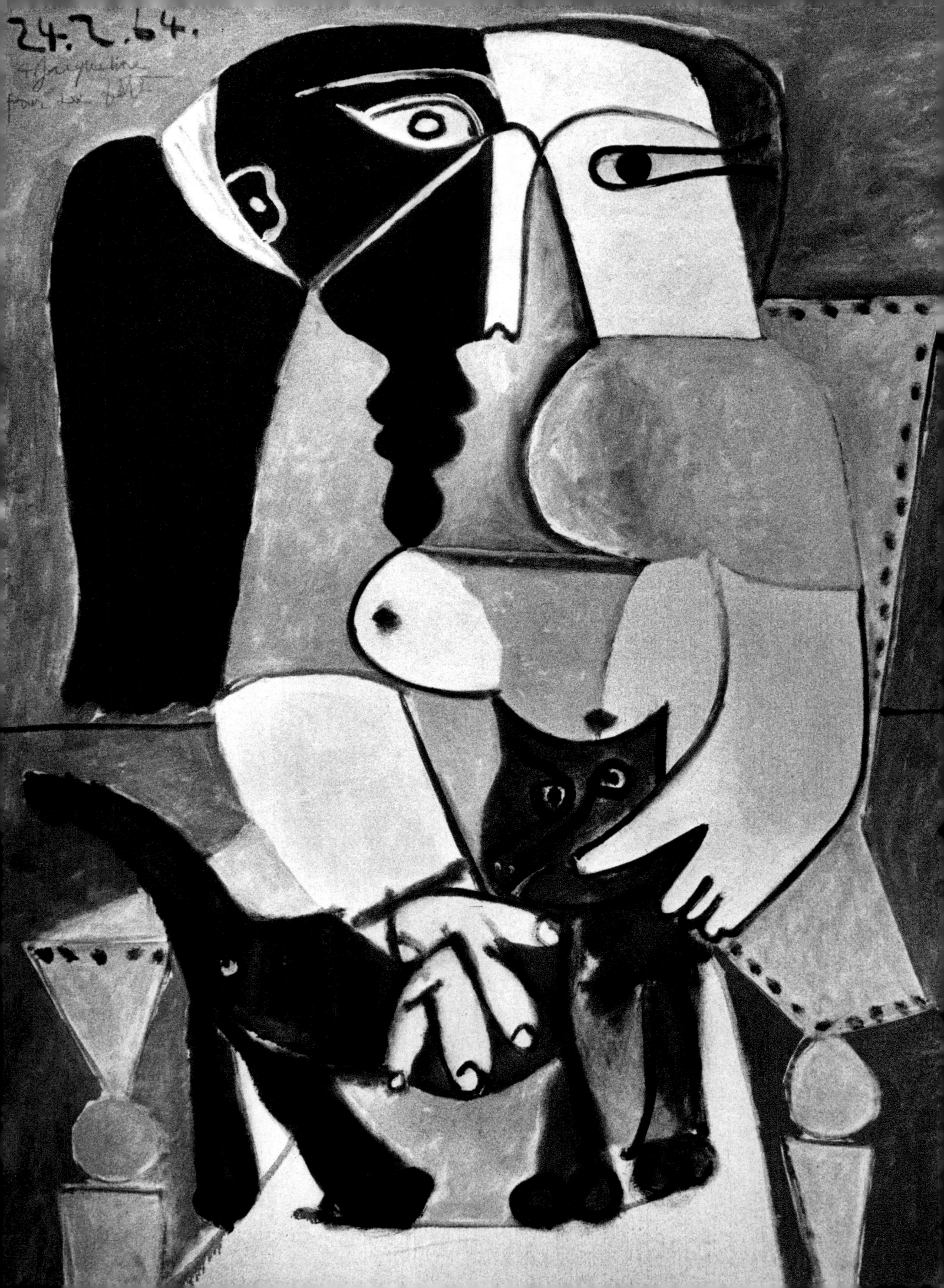
24.2.64.

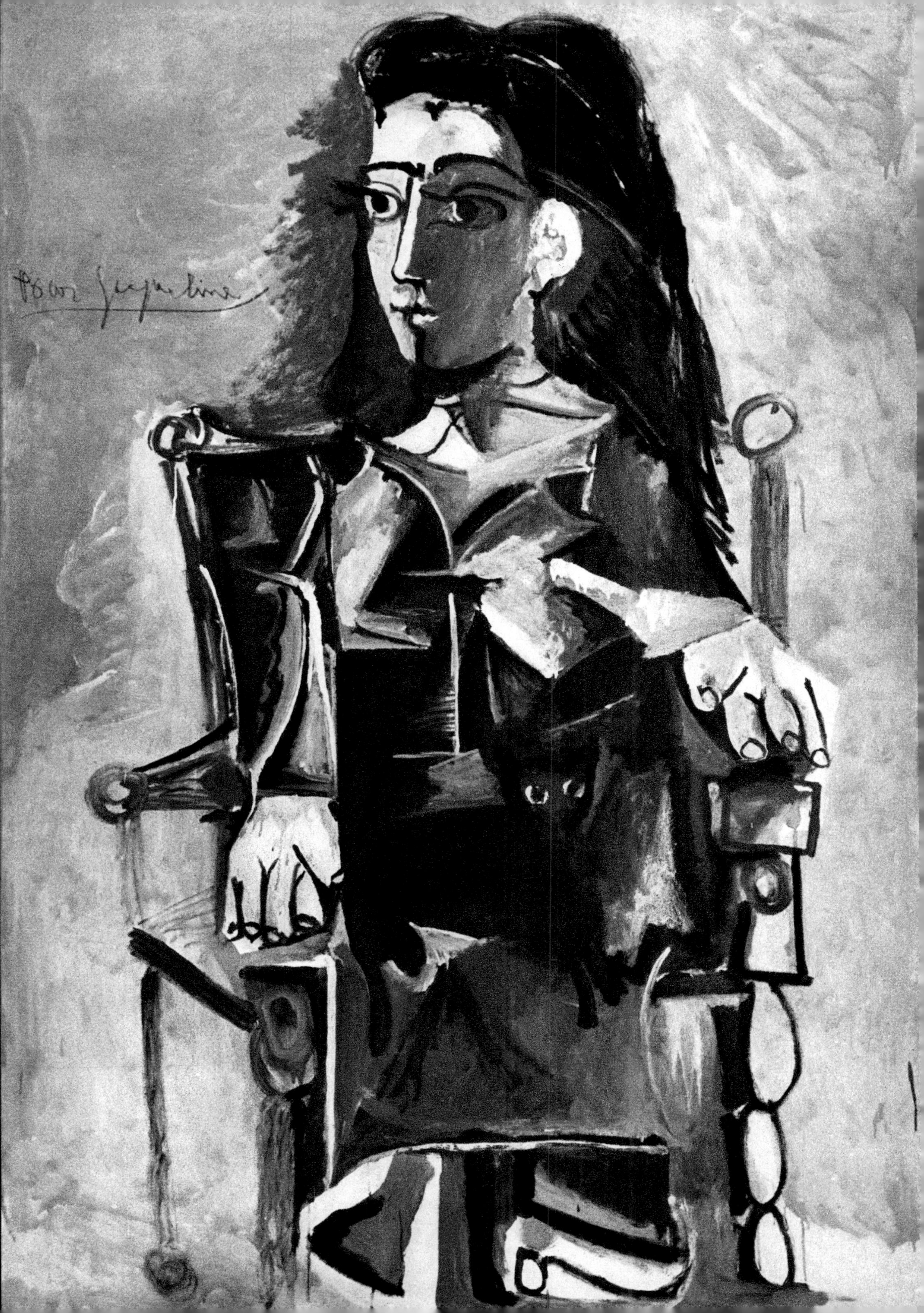
Pour Jacqueline

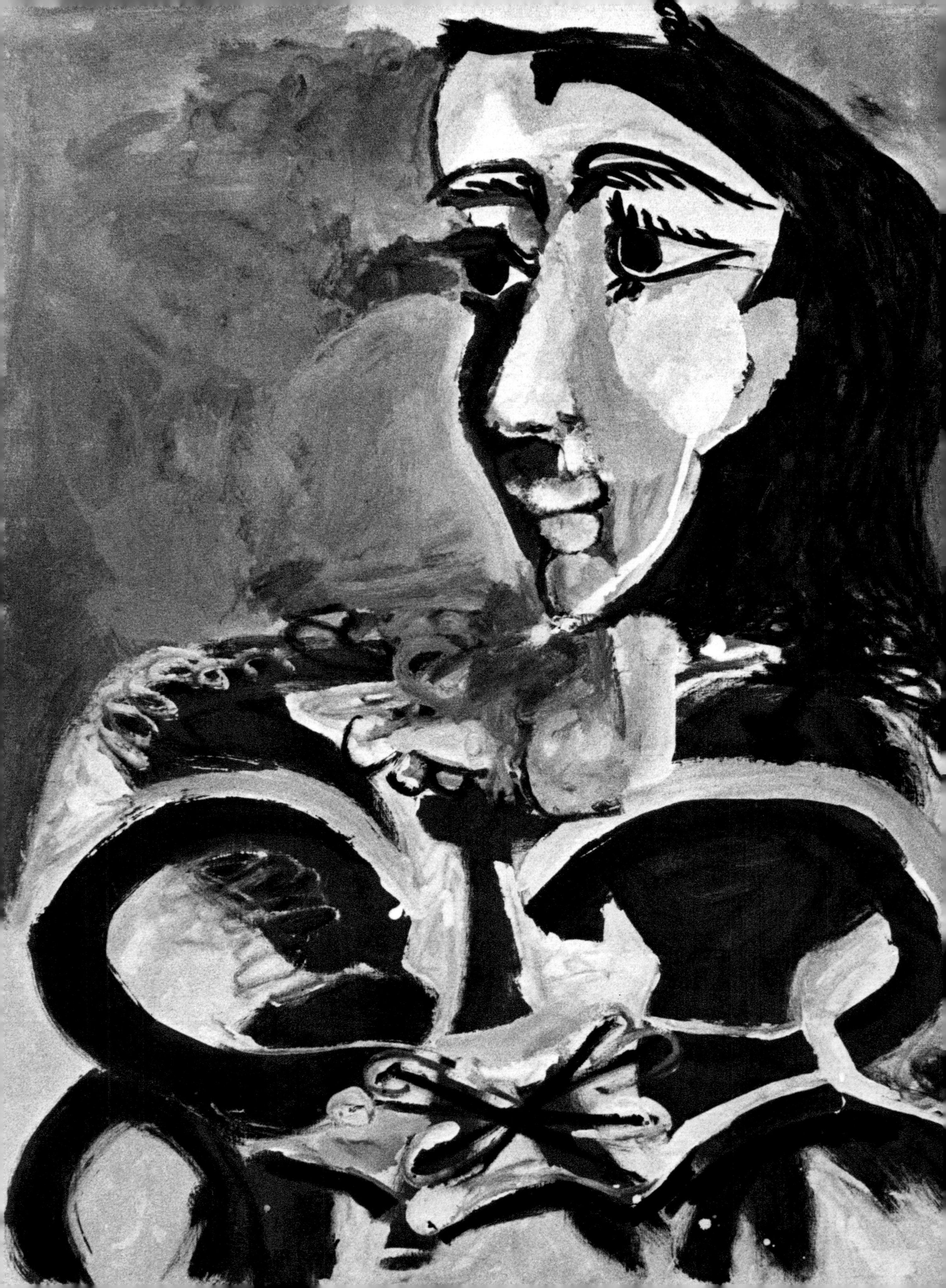

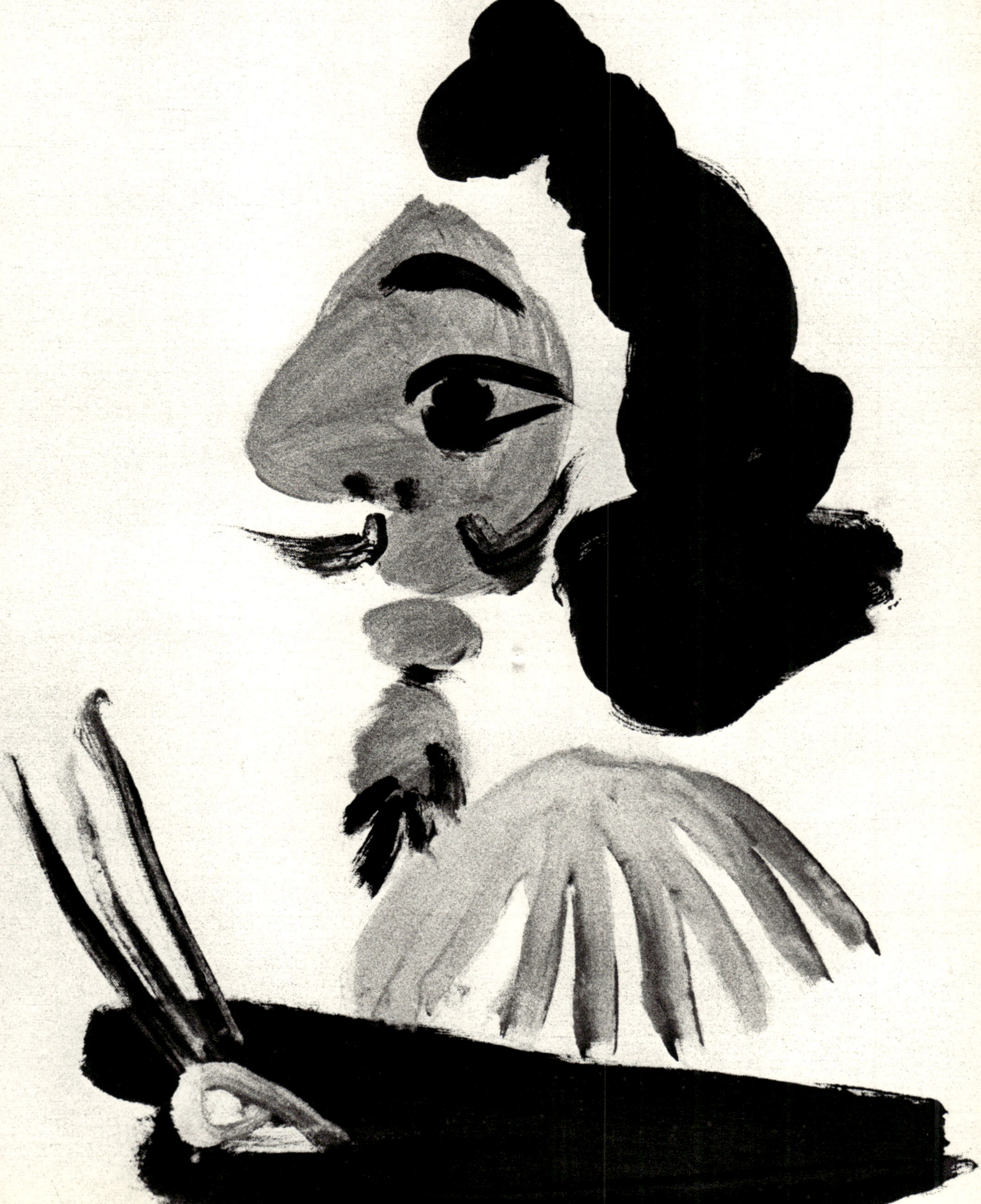

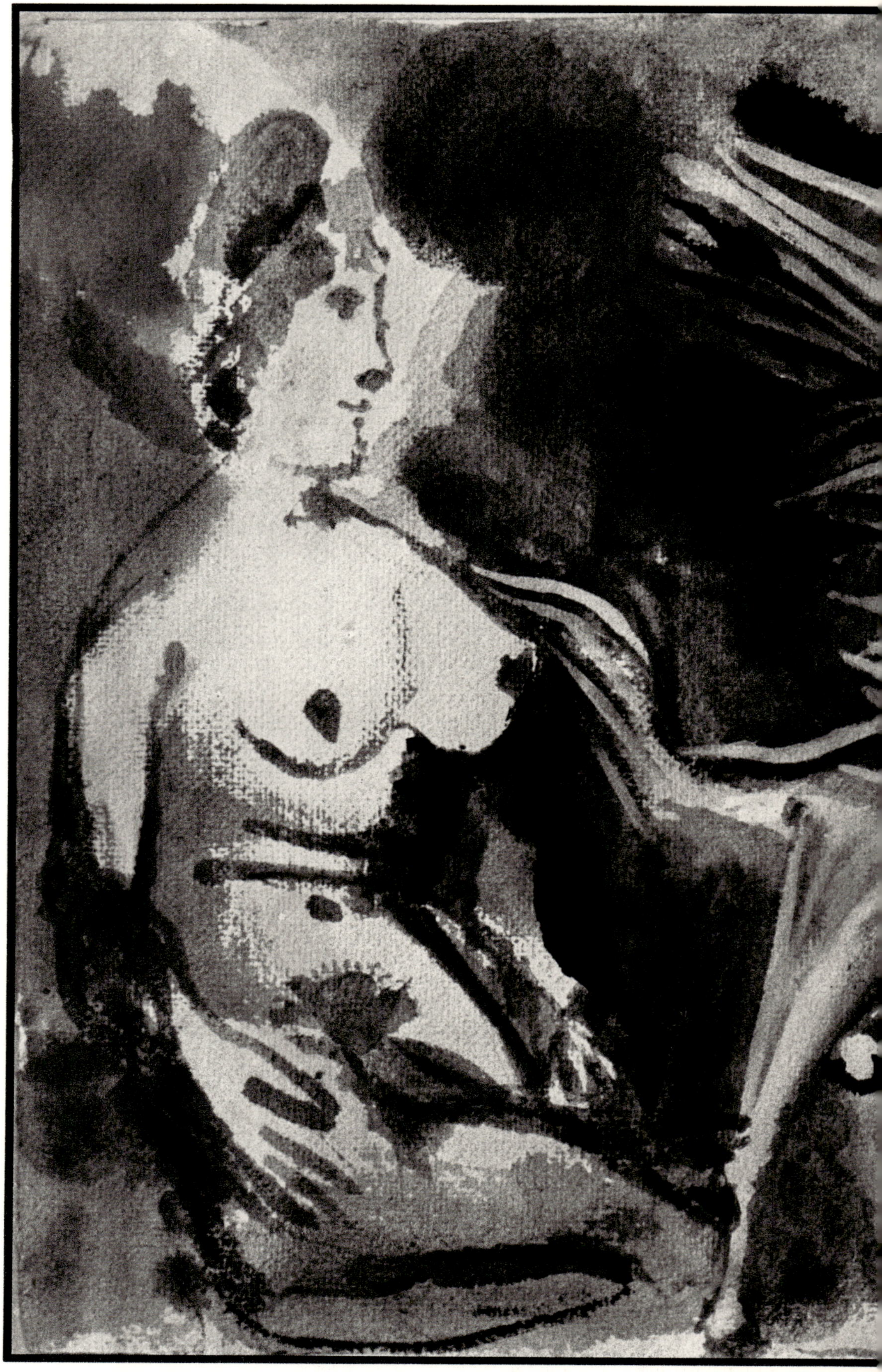

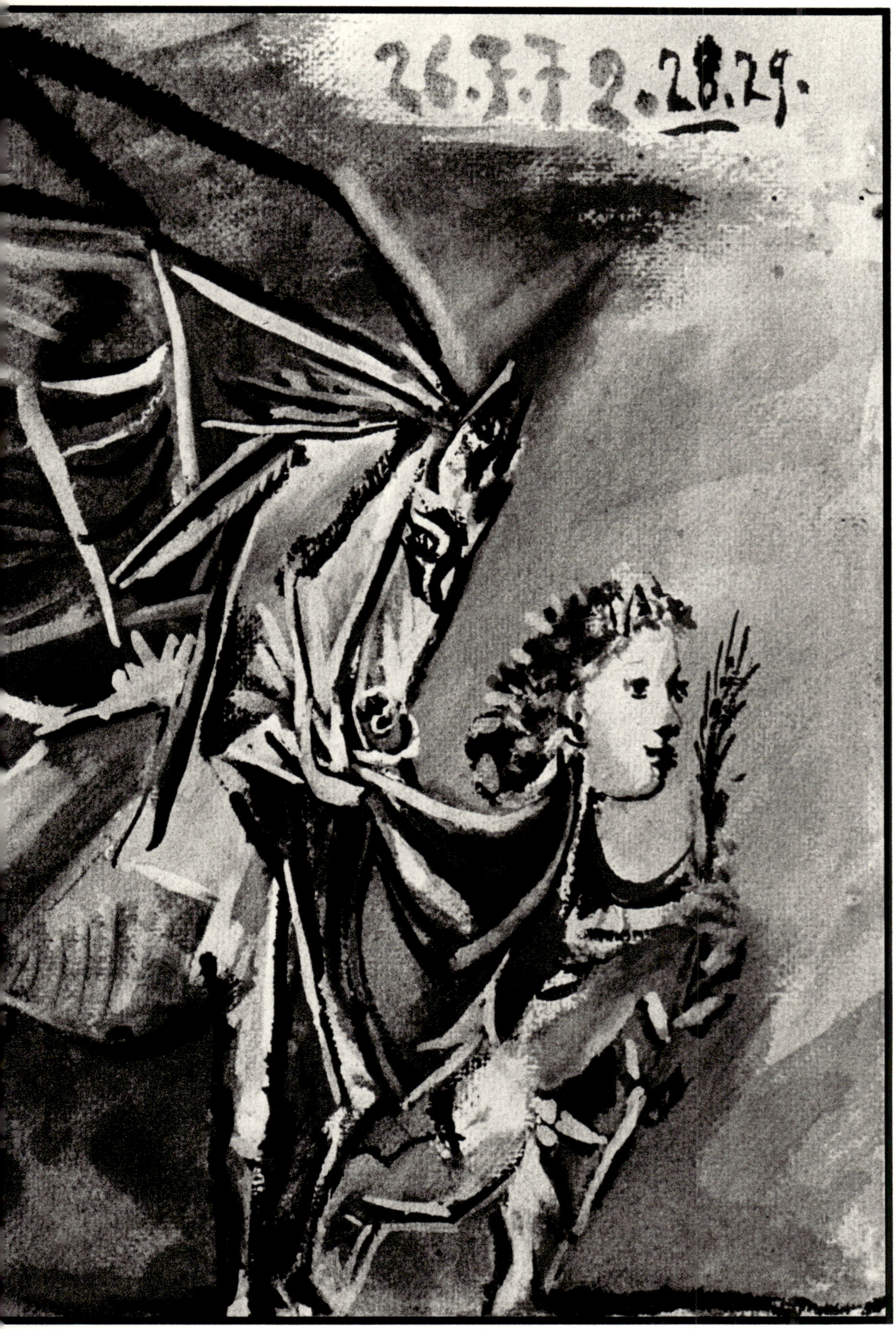

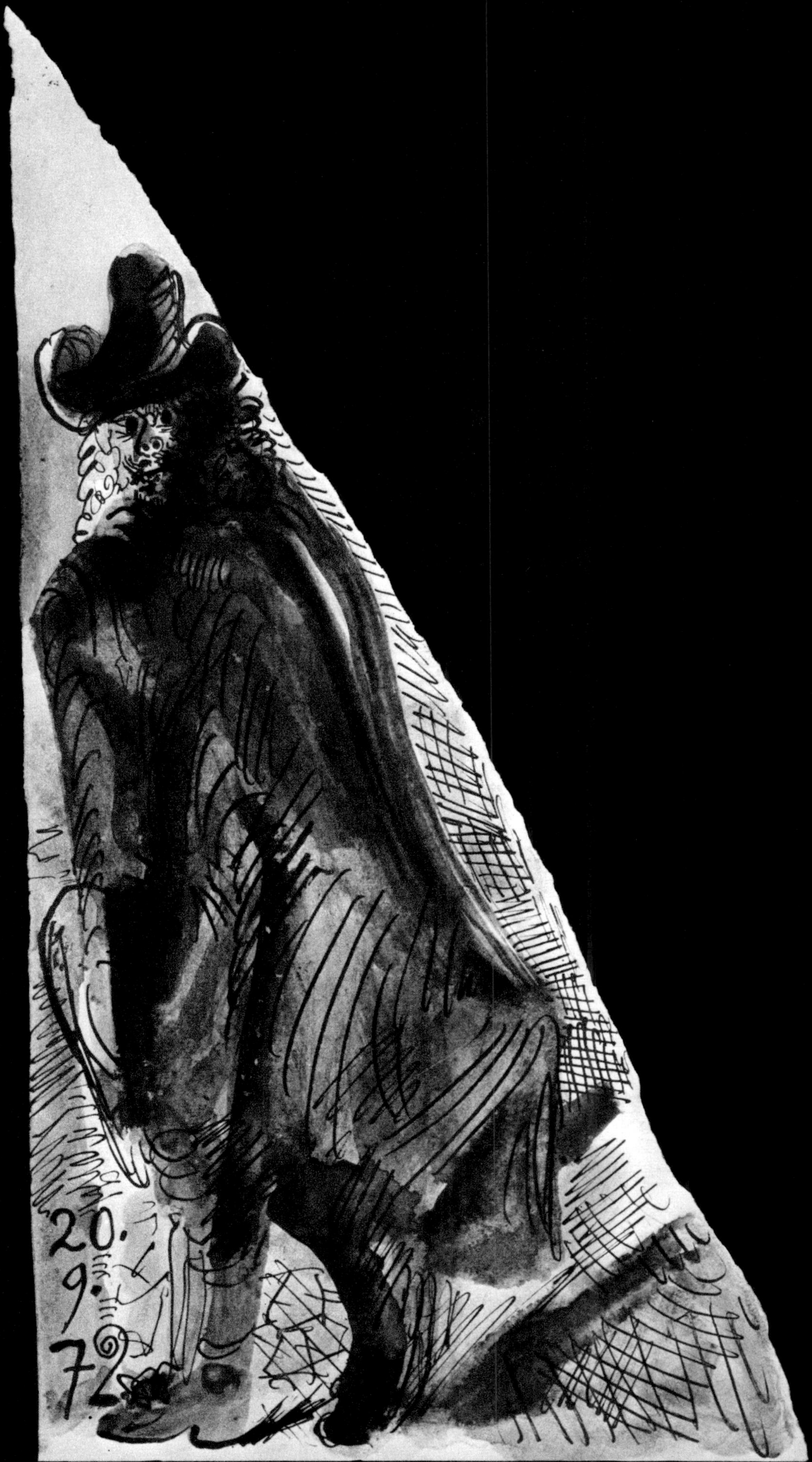
20.
9.
72

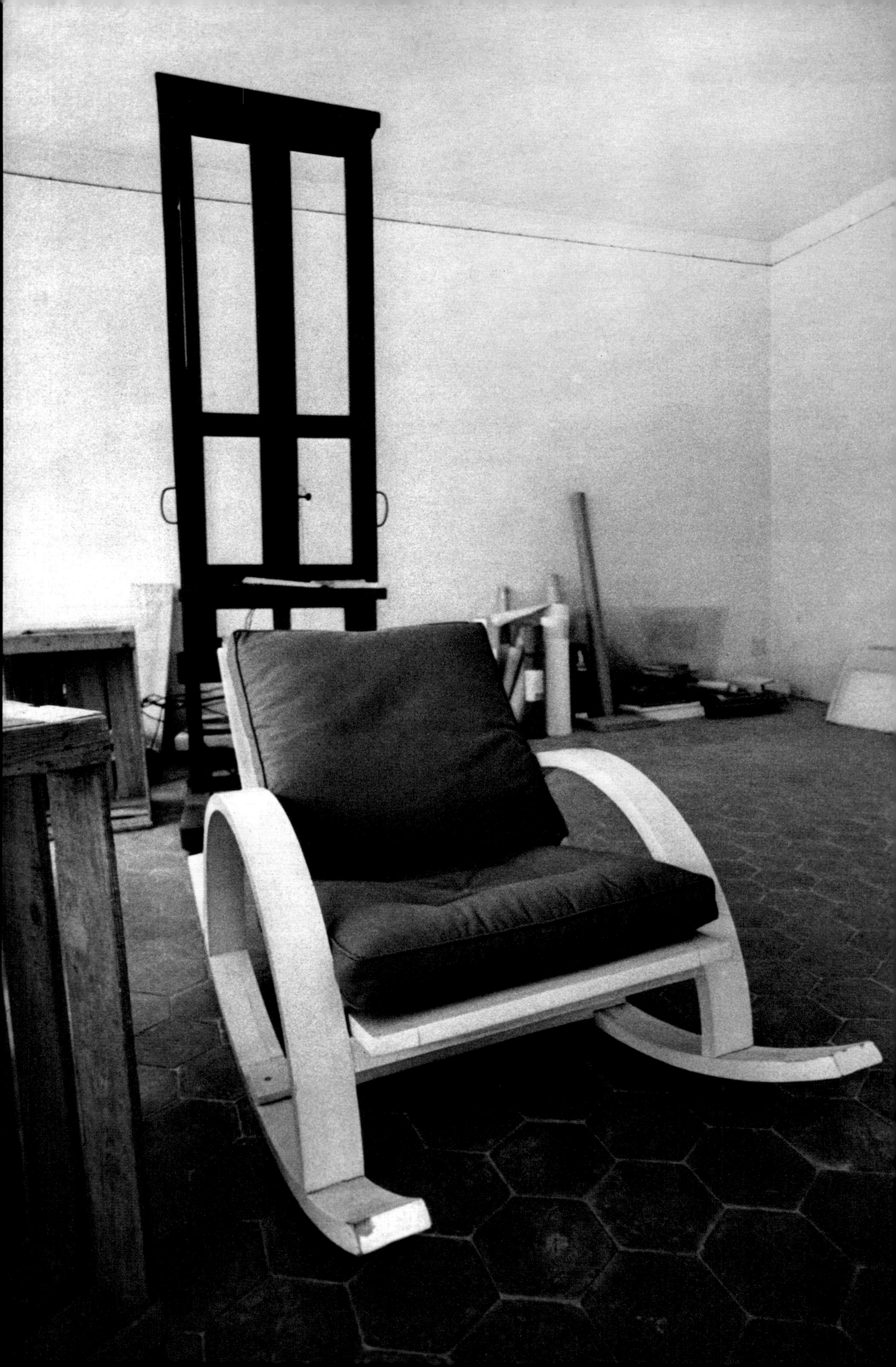

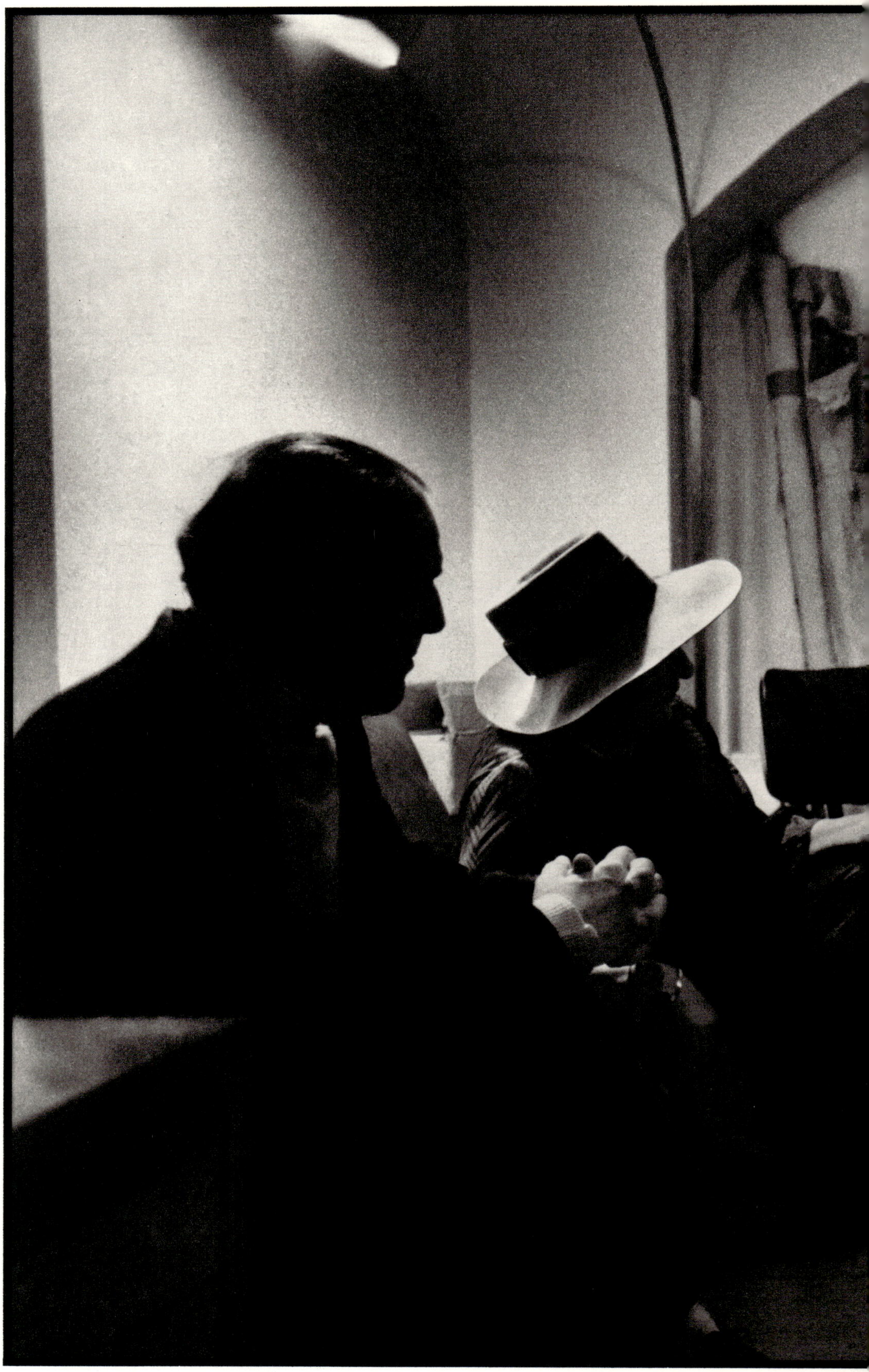

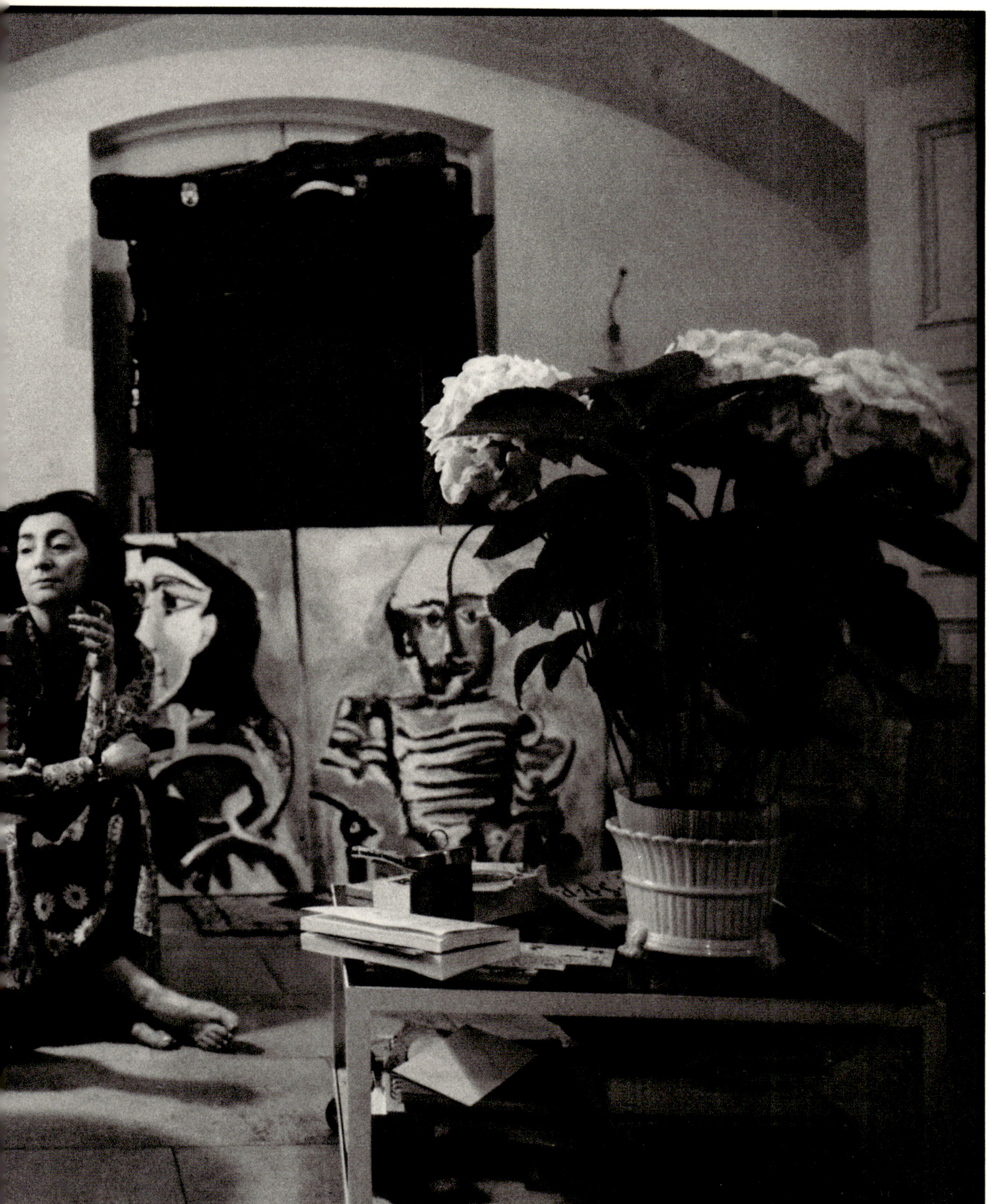

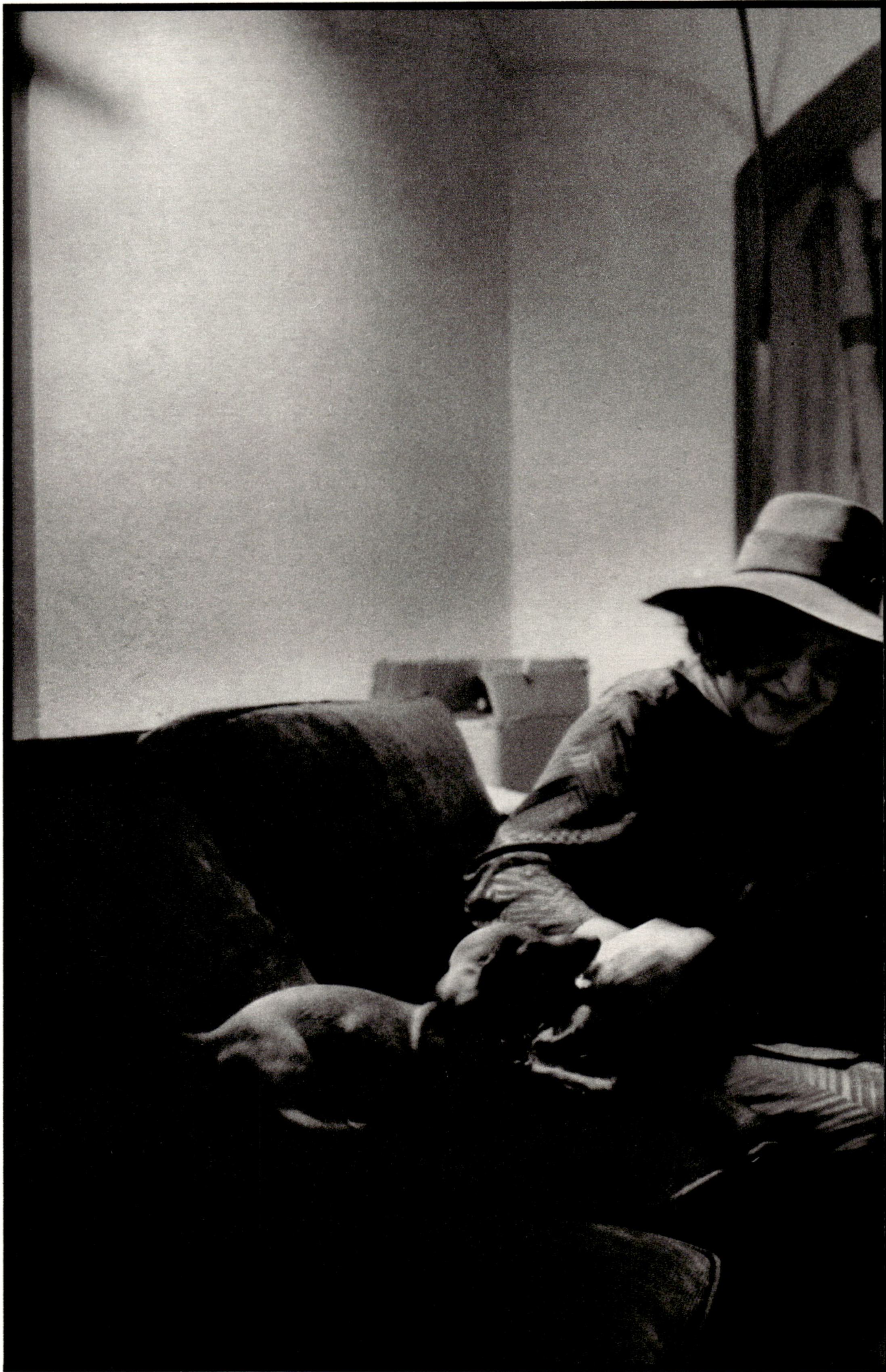

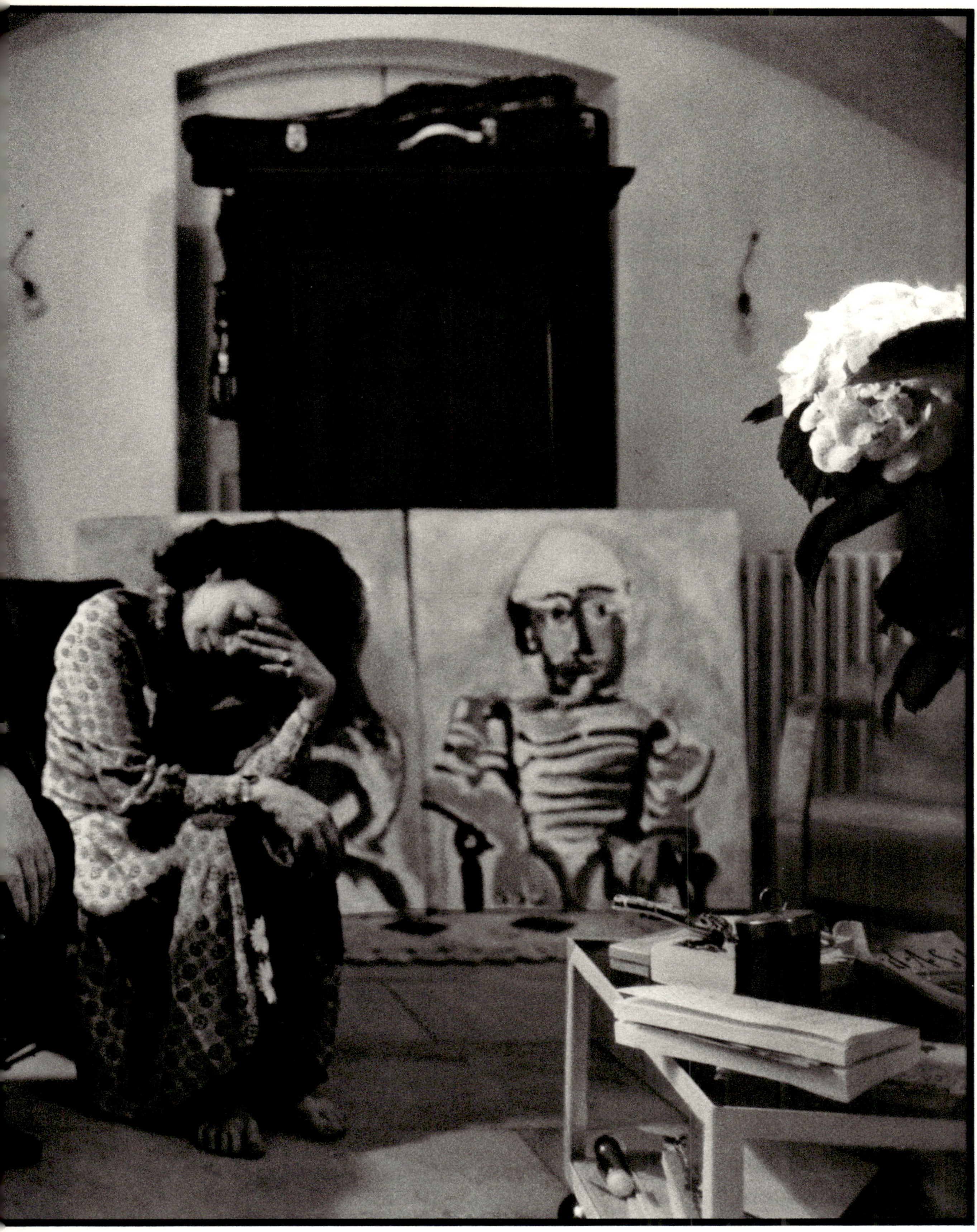

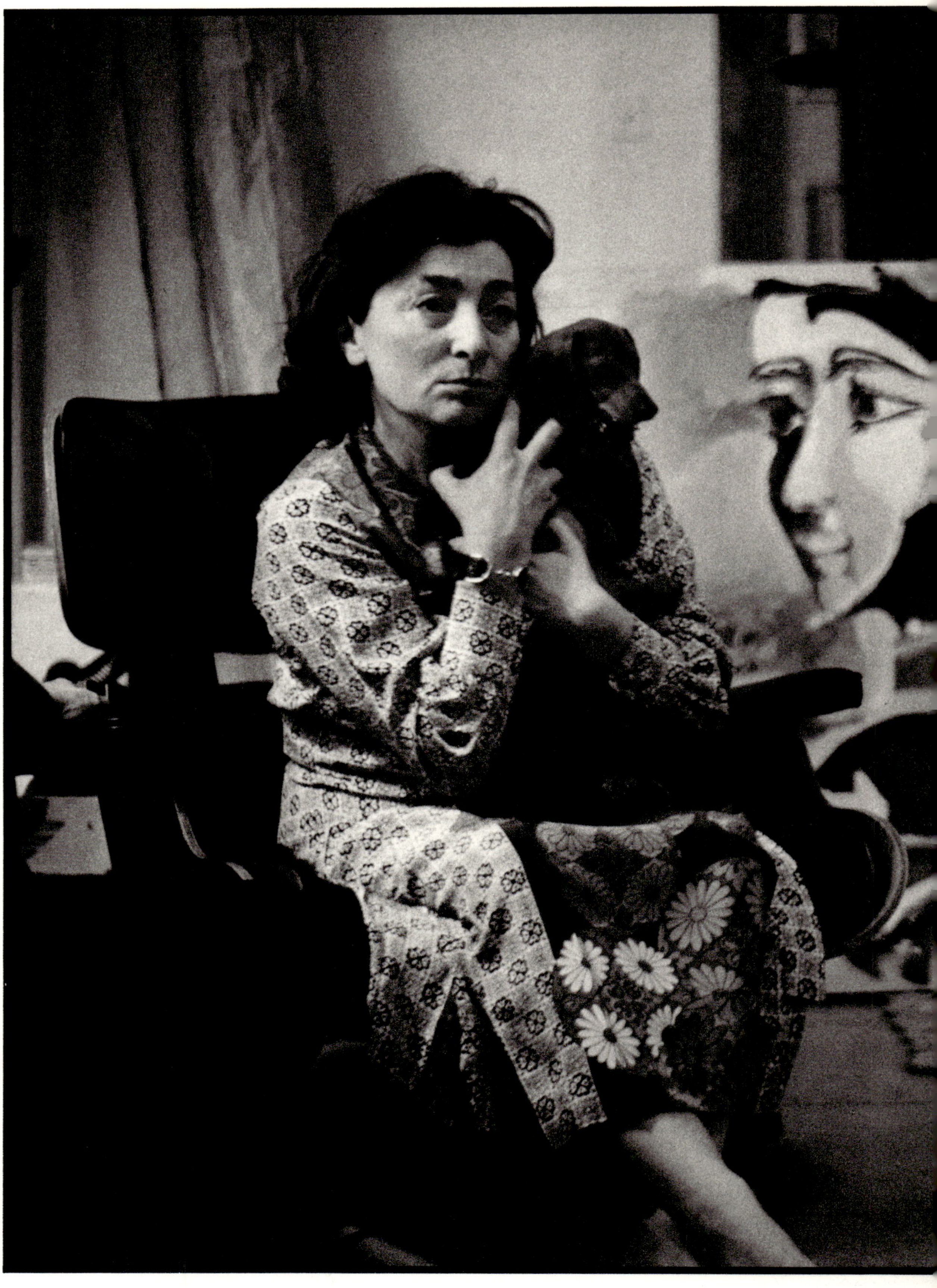

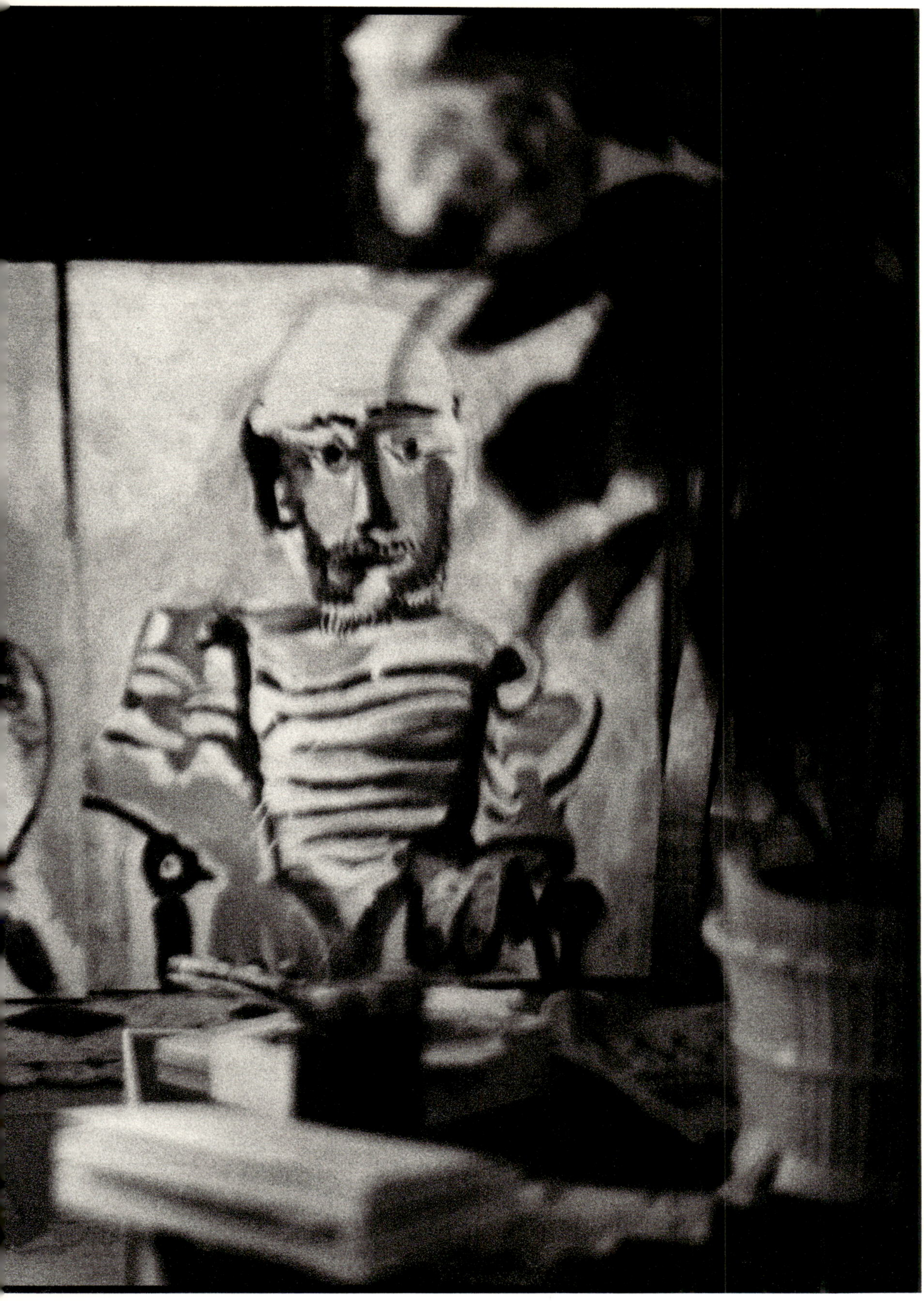

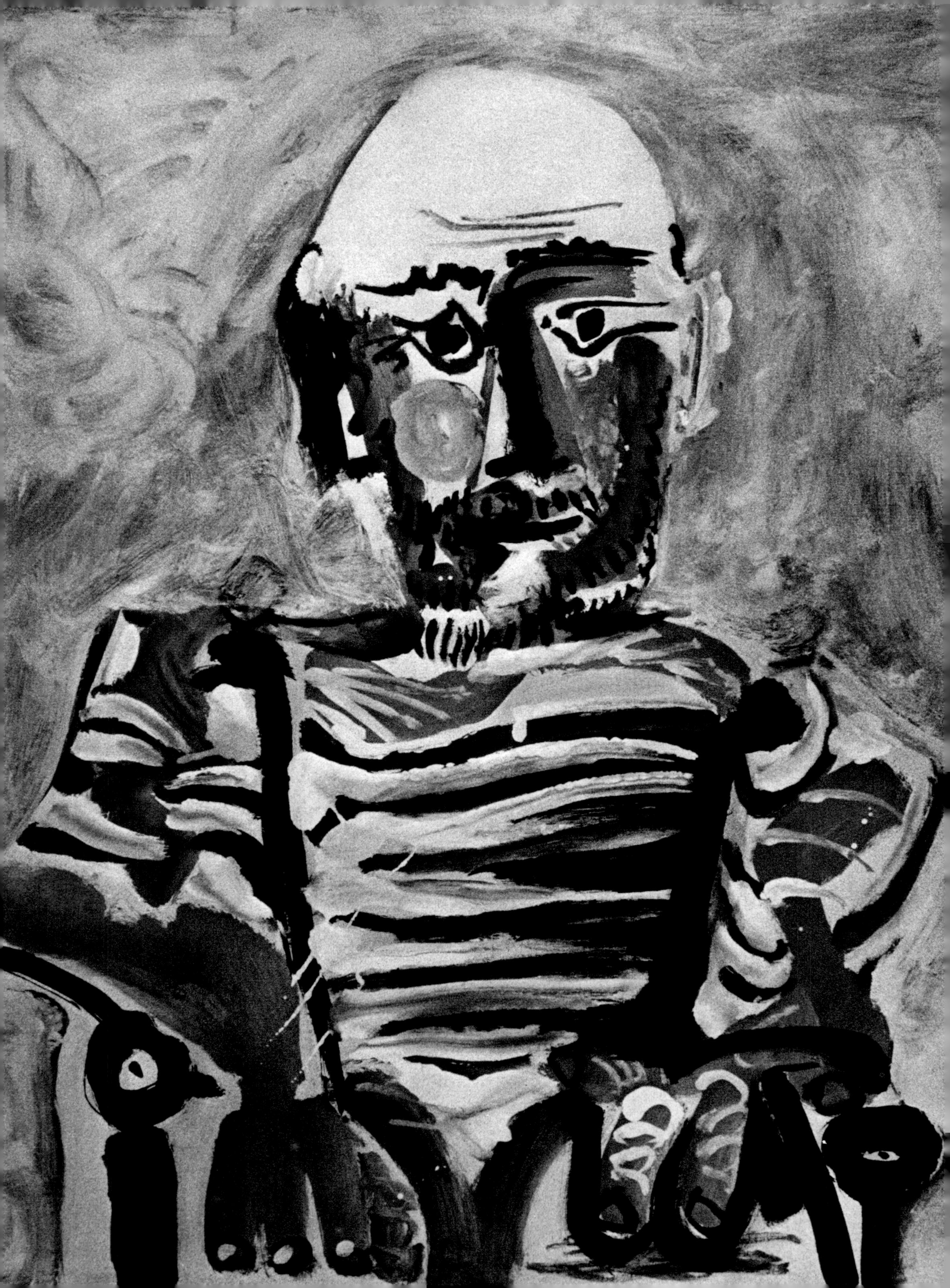

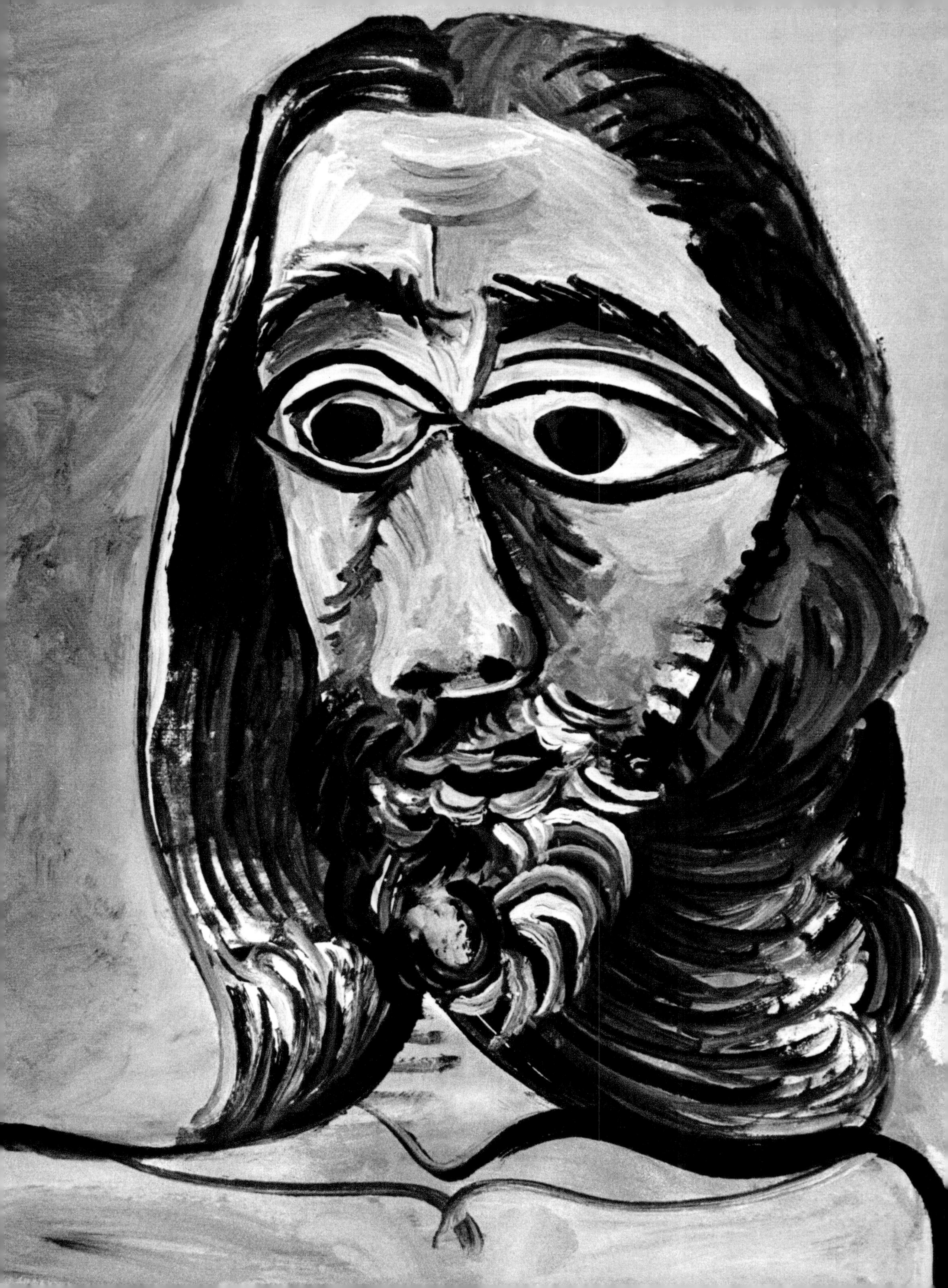

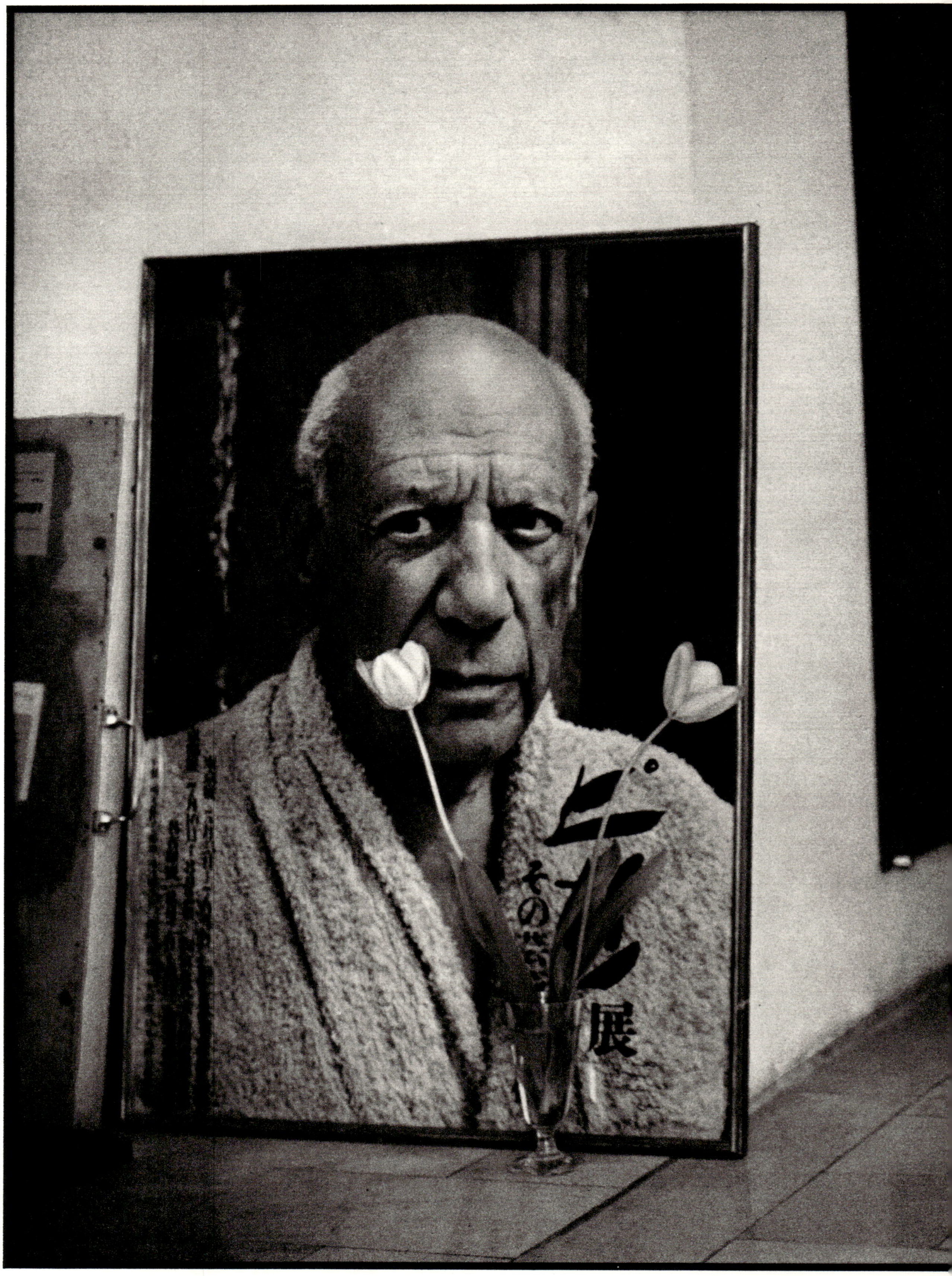
展

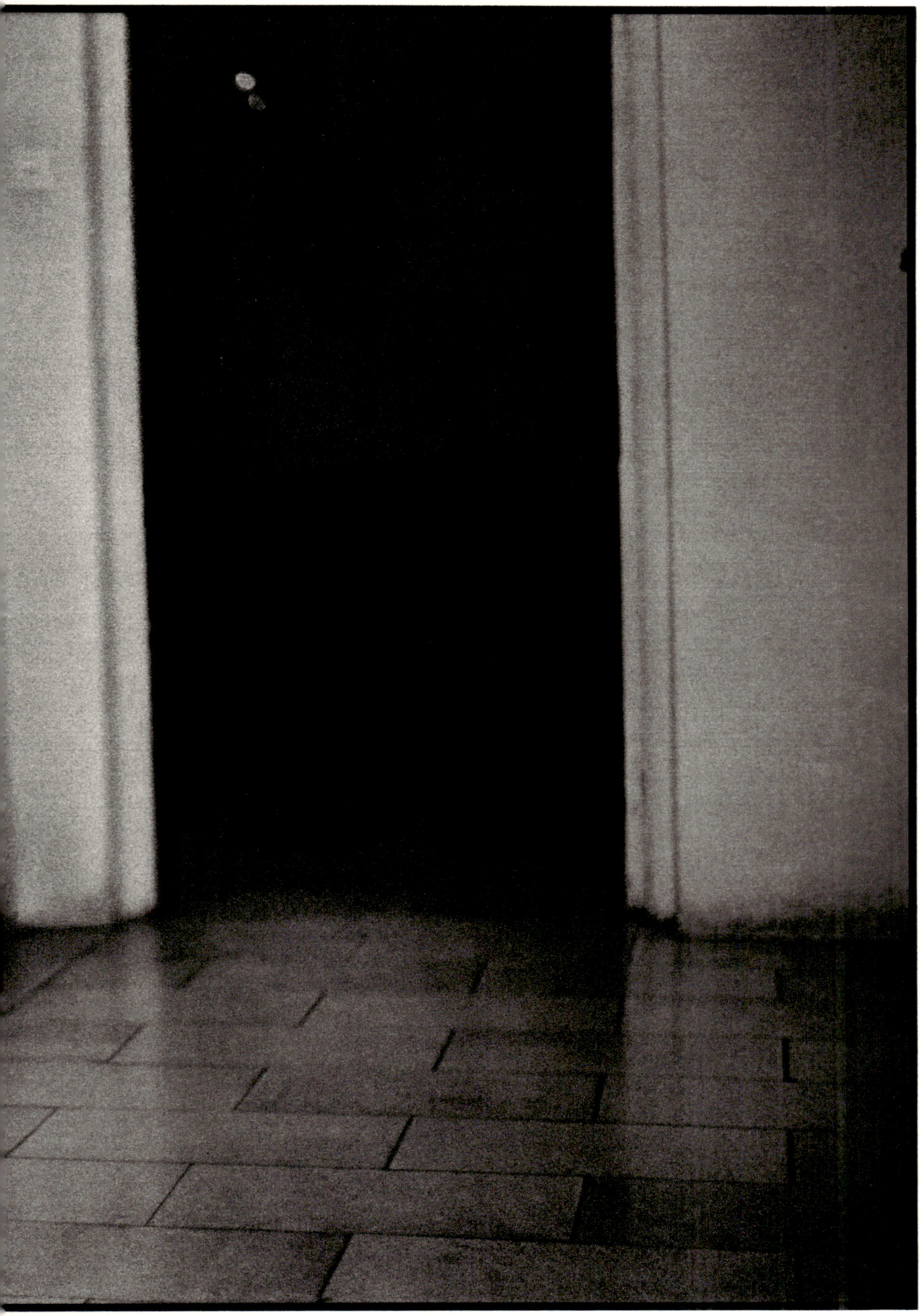

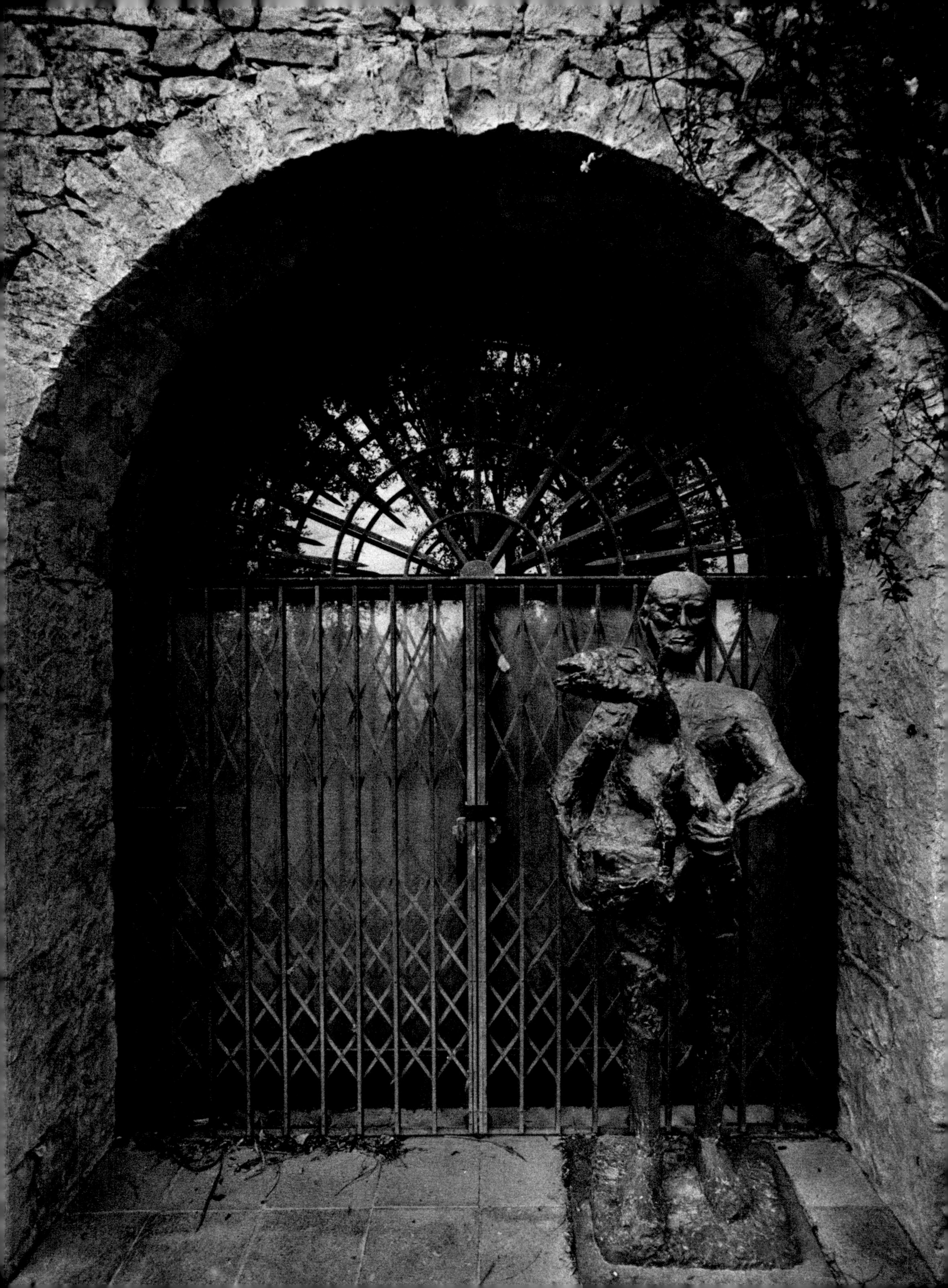

Notre-Dame
de Vie

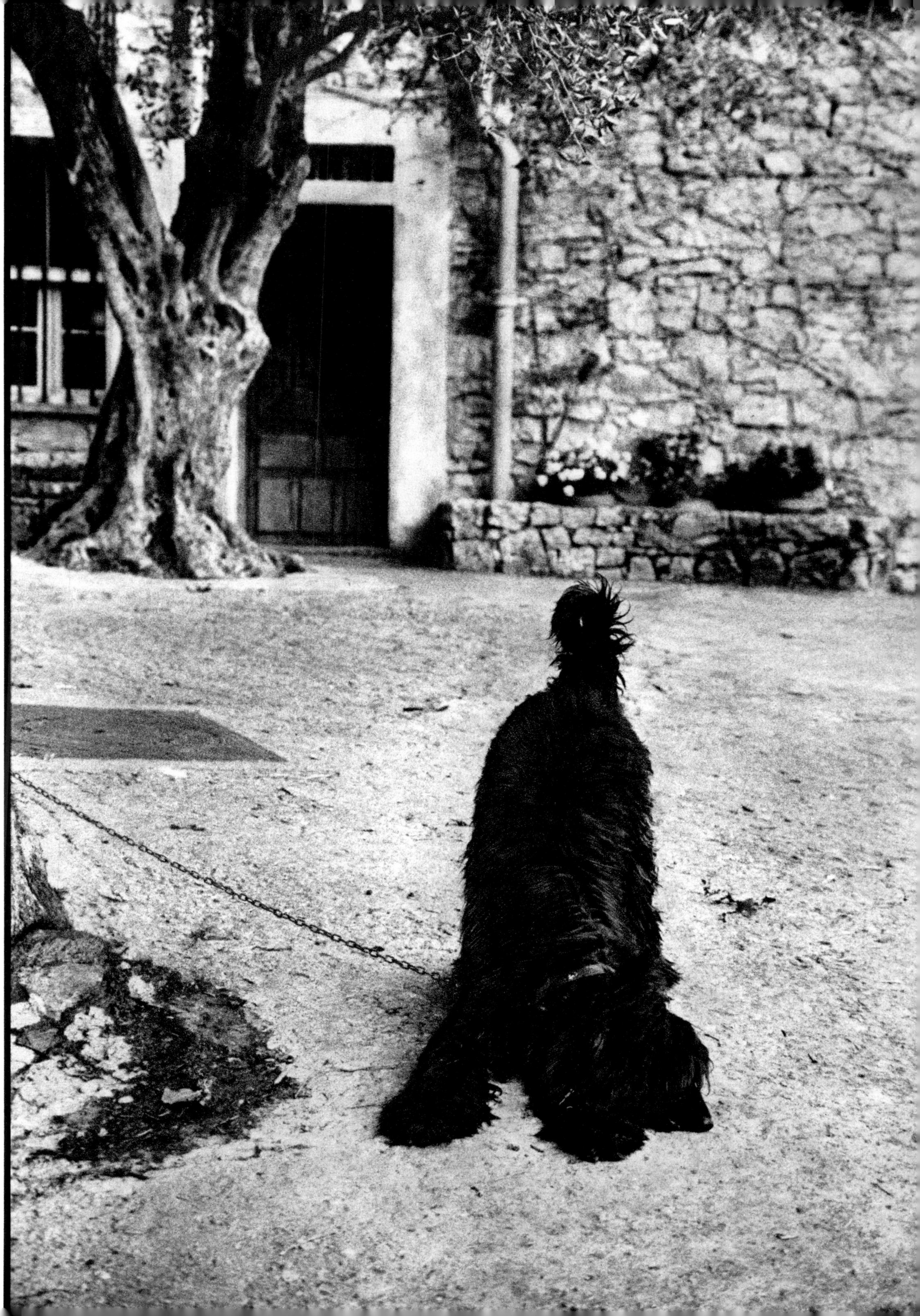

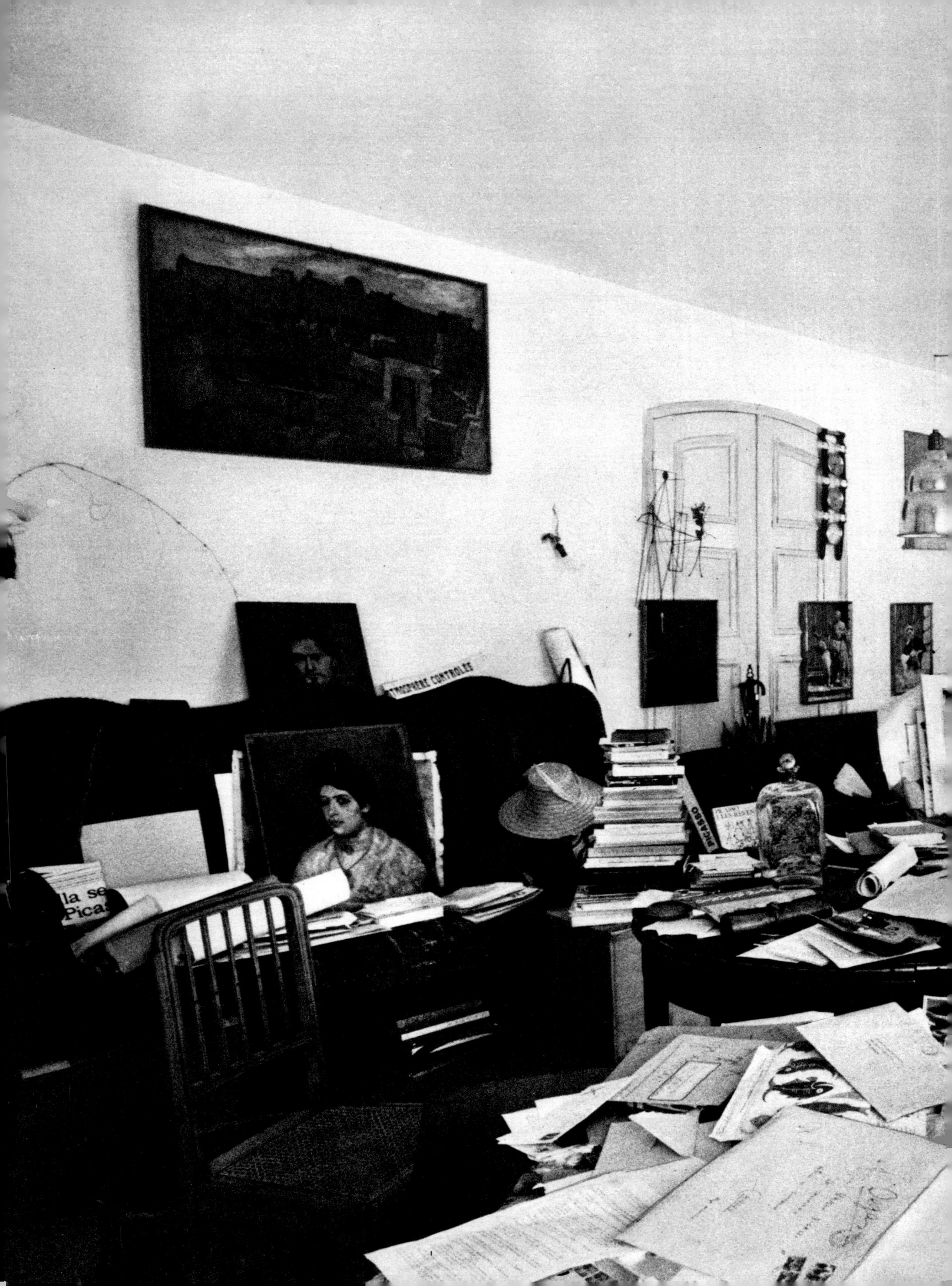
TMOSPHÈRE CONTROLÉE
la se
Picas
PICASSO